To:

_____

From:

_My friend Amla Murphy_

Date:

_12, January 2018_

*Patricia Mitchell*

# EVERYDAY

# *Gifts*

*Spiritual Refreshment*

*for Women*

BARBOUR

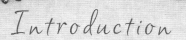

# Introduction

In the routine and busyness of our everyday lives, we often overlook God's many gifts. Ranging from the familiar (how natural to take them for granted!) to the spectacular (how easy to forget who made it possible!), God's goodness surrounds us wherever we are. He continues to offer His gifts, even when we hardly notice.

*Everyday Gifts* is a book of relevant and meaningful devotions inviting you to pause and give thanks for one of God's many blessings. Each day, you will find an uplifting message designed to help you live a gifted life, a life of heightened mindfulness and appreciation of all that God has given to you. As His Spirit continues to work in your heart and mind, He will lead you to deeper spirituality, increased awareness of His presence, and a more vibrant relationship with Him.

Go through the book page by page, or pick out one each day that you would like as your prayer focus. Either way, *Everyday Gifts* is here to bless you as you praise God for all His gifts of goodness and life.

*We all live off his generous bounty, gift after gift after gift.*
JOHN 1:16 MSG

# Contents

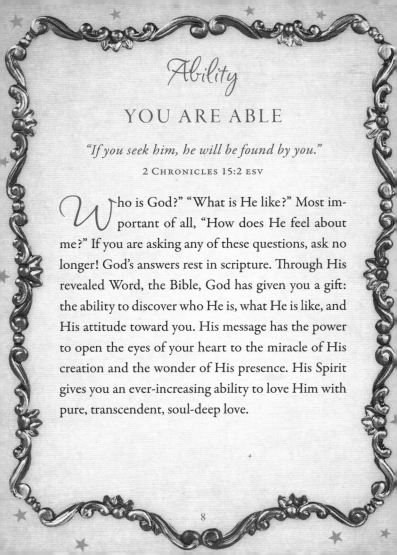

# Ability

## YOU ARE ABLE

*"If you seek him, he will be found by you."*
2 CHRONICLES 15:2 ESV

"Who is God?" "What is He like?" Most important of all, "How does He feel about me?" If you are asking any of these questions, ask no longer! God's answers rest in scripture. Through His revealed Word, the Bible, God has given you a gift: the ability to discover who He is, what He is like, and His attitude toward you. His message has the power to open the eyes of your heart to the miracle of His creation and the wonder of His presence. His Spirit gives you an ever-increasing ability to love Him with pure, transcendent, soul-deep love.

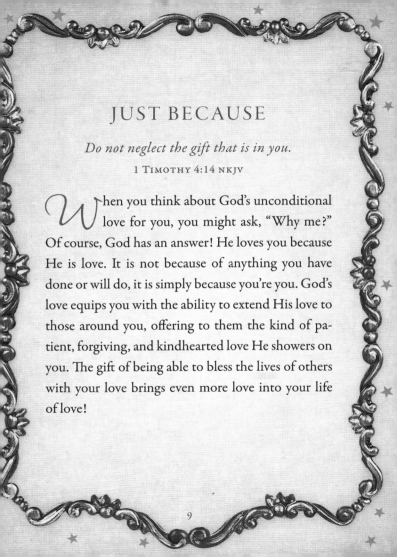

# JUST BECAUSE

*Do not neglect the gift that is in you.*
1 TIMOTHY 4:14 NKJV

When you think about God's unconditional love for you, you might ask, "Why me?" Of course, God has an answer! He loves you because He is love. It is not because of anything you have done or will do, it is simply because you're you. God's love equips you with the ability to extend His love to those around you, offering to them the kind of patient, forgiving, and kindhearted love He showers on you. The gift of being able to bless the lives of others with your love brings even more love into your life of love!

9

# Abundance

## HOW OUTLANDISH!

*My cup runs over.*

PSALM 23:5 NKJV

So you are thinking about God, a heavenly Father who created the world and everything in it. The same sent His Son into the world for the sole purpose of inviting everyone into relationship with Him. What's more, God's Spirit continues to work in the hearts of believers, offering strength and comfort, guidance and protection. How outlandish is that? So are the gifts of faith, grace, kindliness, peace, and mercy that He showers on you with uncommon abundance. You have because He gives and gives, and gives some more. Yes, His abundance could easily be described as completely outlandish!

# PLENTY OF WAYS

*"Who knows but that you have come to your royal position for such a time as this?"*

**ESTHER 4:14 NIV**

One look at the news and you are no doubt struck by the overwhelming number of needs in the world. Yet what often gets lost in the flow of heartbreaking headlines is that there are also an overwhelming number of ways to make things better. Beginning with your thoughts and attitude, words and actions, an abundance of opportunities come across your path every day. It is your heart and your hands that God uses to do His work in your corner of the world, and He has blessed you with everything you need to do it.

# Acceptance

## A SIMPLE GIFT

*Immense in mercy and with an
incredible love, he embraced us.*

EPHESIANS 2:5 MSG

No matter who you are or what you have done or where you have been, God accepts you as His own. His acceptance is a gift He gives; it is not something you or anyone else can earn. In fact, those who try to earn God's acceptance by proving themselves through the things they say and do are missing the whole point! God's acceptance is a gift of grace, and you cannot buy or pay for it. A gift is free, because the giver chooses to give it to you. God chooses to accept you. It's that simple!

# A SACRED PLACE

*Don't you know that you yourselves are God's*
*temple and that God's Spirit dwells in your midst?*
1 CORINTHIANS 3:16 NIV

An old bumper sticker read, "God does not make junk." True then and true now! Every person alive today and who has ever lived has been formed by God and born according to God's plan and purpose. Even more, His Spirit lives in each believing heart and soul. So what does this make you? Not junk, by any means! Your body, accepted by God's Spirit, is a gift from Him, and it deserves the gift of your full acceptance. Your body warrants care and respect, regardless of size, shape, or appearance, for it is a sacred place.

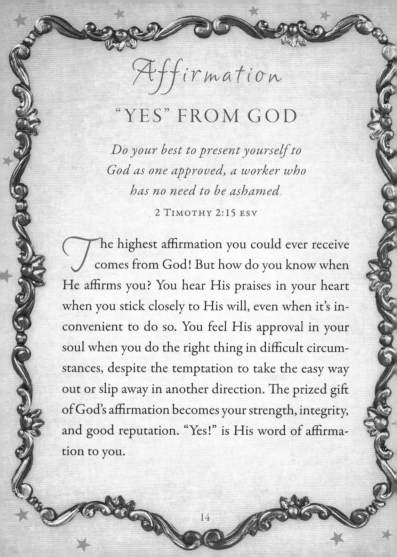

# Affirmation

## "YES" FROM GOD

*Do your best to present yourself to
God as one approved, a worker who
has no need to be ashamed.*

2 TIMOTHY 2:15 ESV

The highest affirmation you could ever receive
comes from God! But how do you know when
He affirms you? You hear His praises in your heart
when you stick closely to His will, even when it's inconvenient to do so. You feel His approval in your
soul when you do the right thing in difficult circumstances, despite the temptation to take the easy way
out or slip away in another direction. The prized gift
of God's affirmation becomes your strength, integrity,
and good reputation. "Yes!" is His word of affirmation to you.

# MAKE A DIFFERENCE

*Encourage each other and*
*give each other strength.*
1 THESSALONIANS 5:11 NCV

When someone pays you a compliment, doesn't it make you feel good? There is nothing like a sincere word of praise to put a glow in your heart and a smile on your face! Compliments show that someone is watching and listening with interest. Affirmations let you know that you're making a difference for the better. That is why, if you want to give someone a gift that won't cost you anything, pay a compliment. Watch. Notice. Find the best, and then say so. Your words may mean more than you'll ever know.

# Beauty

## GOD REVEALED

*The heavens proclaim the glory of God.*
*The skies display his craftsmanship.*

PSALM 19:1 NLT

If you have ever stood on a mountain lookout and gazed across the verdant hills, or watched in reverent silence as the sun splashed a wake of dappled gold across the water before slipping below the horizon, you know. There's more to the world than mere rock, sand, and water! Every part of creation, in its own way, displays the creativity, imagination, and beauty of God. From the smallest blossom in your backyard garden to the farthest star in the universe, God reveals His gifts—and Himself—to you.

# A THING OF BEAUTY

*I am the rose of Sharon,*
*and the lily of the valleys.*
SONG OF SOLOMON 2:1 NKJV

Sometimes it's hard to think of ourselves as beautiful, especially if we compare ourselves to the pictures on glossy magazines or celebrities on TV or in the movies. Yet God's standards are much, much different than what is put before us at supermarket checkouts and theater screens. Rather than searching for flawless skin, the perfect body, or beguiling eyes, He looks at the heart. Where His gifts of faith, goodness, gentleness, kindness, hope, and love are cherished, there He delights in true and lasting beauty!

# Beginnings

## SPIRITUAL BEGINNINGS

*In the beginning was the Word, and the Word
was with God, and the Word was God.*

JOHN 1:1 ESV

You might remember the day you came to faith; or maybe you learned about God as a small child, and you don't recall being without faith. Either way, your faith life had a beginning. That was when God's Spirit started working in your heart, cultivating more and deeper trust in Him as you read, studied, and reflected on scripture. Throughout the seasons of your life, God gives you the gifts of many more beginnings as you apply His Word to your everyday experience. How could today become another gift that deepens and enhances your relationship with Him?

# A NEW LANDSCAPE

*There's an opportune time to do things,*
*a right time for everything on the earth.*

### ECCLESIASTES 3:1 MSG

Passing from one stage of life to the next—say, from married to widowed, or middle age to senior, or strength to disability—we often mourn what we have lost. The years ahead can appear as a barren landscape to our eyes. Yet God is present at every stage of life, and where His presence is, His gift of a new beginning awaits. Though different than what you had known before, His beginnings are for you to take and use. Ask Him to open your eyes to the gifts that await you at the beginning of today and every day.

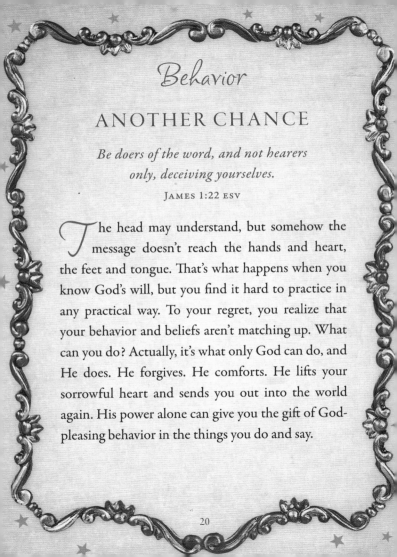

# Behavior

## ANOTHER CHANCE

*Be doers of the word, and not hearers*
*only, deceiving yourselves.*

JAMES 1:22 ESV

The head may understand, but somehow the message doesn't reach the hands and heart, the feet and tongue. That's what happens when you know God's will, but you find it hard to practice in any practical way. To your regret, you realize that your behavior and beliefs aren't matching up. What can you do? Actually, it's what only God can do, and He does. He forgives. He comforts. He lifts your sorrowful heart and sends you out into the world again. His power alone can give you the gift of God-pleasing behavior in the things you do and say.

# GODLY LOVE

*Live a life of love just as Christ loved us.*
EPHESIANS 5:2 NCV

How else could we see, in human terms, God's love if it were not for Jesus? His words and actions showed what love can do. It accepts and understands, embraces and corrects, comforts and heals, rescues and saves. True love—godly love—reveals itself in real and practical application. You see it in behavior that lifts others up and speaks words of kindness and compassion. When you see godly love in action, you know it. When you speak and act with godly love, everyone around you knows it, too. Your behavior comes as God's gift to them.

# Bible

## OPEN TO YOU

*"Hey there! All who are thirsty, come to the water!*
*Are you penniless? Come anyway—buy and eat!"*
ISAIAH 55:1 MSG

The clear message of God's love for you rings clearly throughout the Bible. You read how God guided His people and provided for them as they traveled life's path, making their way through deserts of unbelief and struggle, and standing on the summit of enlightenment and revelation. Like a loving parent, God admonishes those who go astray, calling them back to Him with a loud and strong voice. The Bible is God's gift to you and to all who want to know Him and who wish to worship Him. It is open to all—open to you.

# GOD'S INSPIRED WORD

*All Scripture is breathed out by God.*

2 TIMOTHY 3:16 ESV

The Holy Spirit guided the hands and hearts of those He called as writers of scripture. After prayerful study of these writings on the part of believers throughout the centuries, we possess an extraordinary gift, the Bible. Each book of the Bible is intended to enhance, enlighten, and elevate your spiritual understanding and designed to strengthen your faith and knowledge of God. Though some passages lie shrouded in mystery, all parts of the Bible are God's inspired Word and well worth your time and attention. How will you let His gift bless you today?

# Blessings

## THE ANSWER IS YES

*This is the confidence that we have in Him, that if we ask anything according to His will, He hears us.*

1 JOHN 5:14 NKJV

There is one request you can take to God and know ahead of time that His answer will be "Yes!" Ask for the gift of spiritual blessings that concern your soul's salvation; He is delighted to comply. A prayer for stronger confidence in Jesus' life, death, and resurrection, for example, brings faith-lifting results. Perhaps you would discover more opportunities to hear His Word, spend more time meditating on His Gospel message, or realize a biblical truth formerly closed to you. In whatever way God chooses to bless you, His answer to this kind of prayer is always "Yes."

# HE UNDERSTANDS

*Do not worry about anything, but pray and ask
God for everything you need, always giving thanks.*

### Philippians 4:6 NCV

Jesus' earthly ministry gives proof to the fact that
God cares about our physical needs. When He
walked among people, He bestowed the blessings of
bodily healing on those who asked. He was moved
with compassion for those who were hungry, and He
fed them. At times, He Himself felt tired, hurt, hungry, thirsty, dejected, and sad. In Jesus, you know that
God understands your deepest feelings and most
pressing needs. Take each one to Him in prayer, and
wait on Him to answer with a gift that gives honor to
Him and richly blesses you.

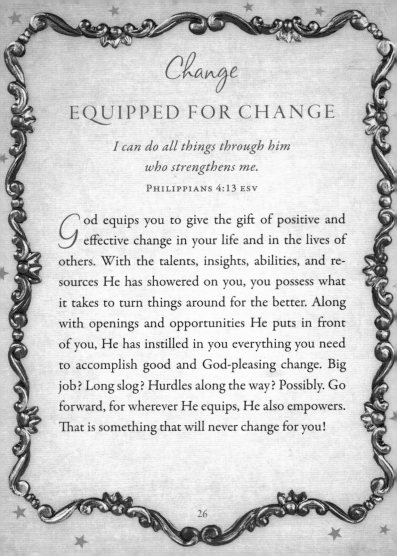

# Change

## EQUIPPED FOR CHANGE

*I can do all things through him
who strengthens me.*

PHILIPPIANS 4:13 ESV

God equips you to give the gift of positive and effective change in your life and in the lives of others. With the talents, insights, abilities, and resources He has showered on you, you possess what it takes to turn things around for the better. Along with openings and opportunities He puts in front of you, He has instilled in you everything you need to accomplish good and God-pleasing change. Big job? Long slog? Hurdles along the way? Possibly. Go forward, for wherever He equips, He also empowers. That is something that will never change for you!

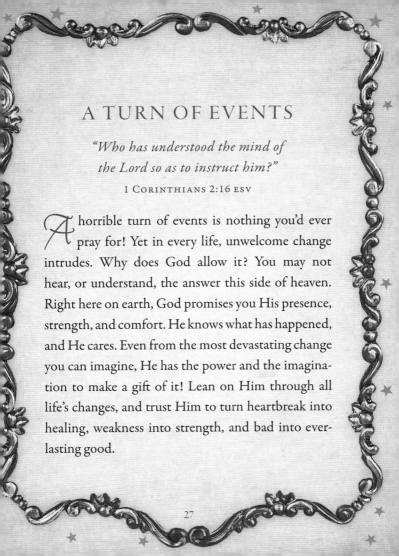

# A TURN OF EVENTS

*"Who has understood the mind of the Lord so as to instruct him?"*

1 Corinthians 2:16 esv

A horrible turn of events is nothing you'd ever pray for! Yet in every life, unwelcome change intrudes. Why does God allow it? You may not hear, or understand, the answer this side of heaven. Right here on earth, God promises you His presence, strength, and comfort. He knows what has happened, and He cares. Even from the most devastating change you can imagine, He has the power and the imagination to make a gift of it! Lean on Him through all life's changes, and trust Him to turn heartbreak into healing, weakness into strength, and bad into everlasting good.

# Choice

## CHOOSE TODAY

*"If you decide that it's a bad thing to worship GOD, then choose a god you'd rather serve—and do it today."*

JOSHUA 24:15 MSG

Out of His boundless love for you, God has chosen you as His own. Yet He forces no one to choose Him, love Him in return, or live in obedience to His commandments. Instead, He gives to each person the gift of choice. If you haven't chosen Him yet, God's invitation remains open, and He desires you to embrace Him as your true and only God. Let your good choice fill your heart with love toward Him, and express itself in the way you think, speak, and act. He has made His choice! How about you?

# THE BETTER WAY

*You say, "I am allowed to do anything"—*
*but not everything is good for you.*
1 Corinthians 6:12 NLT

In our society, we cherish the freedom, and that of others, to choose our personal beliefs, opinions, and lifestyles without undue restriction. Even though many things are permissible and acceptable by human standards, however, not everything is right for us to do. God's time-honored rules and guidelines are meant to help us grow spiritually mature so we can enjoy inner peace and delight in a close relationship with Him. When it comes to what is allowed by society but not by God in His Word, you have a choice. Choose the better way—His way.

# Church

## A PLACE OF PRAYER

*I was glad when they said to me,*
*"Let us go into the house of the LORD."*

PSALM 122:1 NKJV

If you have ever tried to be on the go 24/7, you probably have found it doesn't work—not for long, anyway. You end up tired, stressed, and unable to enjoy whatever you gained by pushing your endurance to the limit. That is why Sabbath rest is vital. When you enter His sanctuary, it is one place where your focus centers completely on God. As you hear His Word, sing His praises, and offer your prayers, He refreshes your spirit and renews your heart. Church is far from simply an obligation; it is a gift from God to you.

# YOU ARE THE GIFT

*We are many,*
*but in Christ we are all one body.*

ROMANS 12:5 NCV

God serves you in church, and at the same time, you serve those around you. Your presence sets a positive example of putting Him ahead of pressing to-dos or other activities. You also serve others by contributing talents, abilities, and resources needed to build a living and lively congregation. You put yourself among a group of believers willing and able to welcome others, apply God's Word to daily living, and make a difference in the community. While your church is God's gift to you, never doubt that you are God's gift to your church.

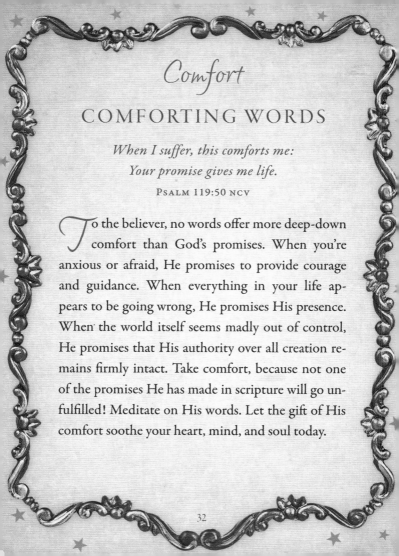

# *Comfort*

## COMFORTING WORDS

*When I suffer, this comforts me:*
*Your promise gives me life.*

**PSALM 119:50 NCV**

To the believer, no words offer more deep-down comfort than God's promises. When you're anxious or afraid, He promises to provide courage and guidance. When everything in your life appears to be going wrong, He promises His presence. When the world itself seems madly out of control, He promises that His authority over all creation remains firmly intact. Take comfort, because not one of the promises He has made in scripture will go unfulfilled! Meditate on His words. Let the gift of His comfort soothe your heart, mind, and soul today.

# IN TROUBLED TIMES

*"I, I am he who comforts you."*
ISAIAH 51:12 ESV

When something wonderful happens in your life, no doubt you're eager to share the good news with family and friends. Their happiness for you adds to your joy! Similarly, when difficulties come your way, you want to talk about the situation and your feelings with people who mean the most to you. Their understanding and encouragement ease your burden and often light the way ahead. Their thoughts and prayers, care and concern, help and support are among God's many ways of bringing you the gift of comfort in troubled times.

# Commandments

## A CLEAR LOOK

*I would not have known what sin was had it not been for the law.*

ROMANS 7:7 NIV

It's unpleasant to admit shortcomings. It is so unpleasant, in fact, that some of us prefer not to think too often about them, or brush them off as mere idiosyncrasies. However, unless we're willing to take a clear-eyed look at our shortcomings—our sins—we will never experience the depth of God's forgiveness. Without experiencing the depth of God's forgiveness, we will never know the height of living freely and joyfully as forgiven children of God. His commandments, found in His Word, reflect our shortcomings as nothing else can. To realize the gift of God's forgiveness, receive the gift of His commandments.

# WAY TO GO

*Great peace have those who love Your law,*
*and nothing causes them to stumble.*

PSALM 119:165 NKJV

Mention God's commandments, and the phrase "you shall not" most often comes to mind. Yet with every "shall not," there's a "shall." God's commandments, by warning us what to avoid, also tell us what He would have us to do. We shall not curse, so we shall use our words to bless. We shall not steal, so we shall protect what belongs to others. We shall not envy, so we shall rest content with what we have. In God's commandments, we possess two gifts: one warns us away from sin, the other turns us toward Him.

# Compassion

## COMPASSION IN ACTION

*When he saw them coming, he was overcome*
*with pity and healed their sick.*

MATTHEW 14:14 MSG

Whenever Jesus saw people suffering in body or soul, He was moved with overwhelming compassion. His compassion went beyond feelings of pity or sadness—His compassion took action. He healed. He fed. He forgave. He embraced the humble of heart. That's the kind of compassion that God has for you. When you come to Him with a need, when you lay your burdens before Him, when you plead with Him to give you direction, you will receive the gift of His compassion—compassion that takes action in your life. In what way could His compassion work for you today?

# PRACTICAL COMPASSION

*"This is what the LORD All-Powerful says:*
*'Do what is right and true.*
*Be kind and merciful to each other.'"*

ZECHARIAH 7:9 NCV

God's compassion for you compels Him to help you in meaningful ways. Say you're troubled: He may strengthen you in faith so you can go forward with confidence. He will infuse you with His Spirit so you can respond effectively to your circumstances. He may also choose to offer to you new opportunities to grow and thrive. When the compassion you feel for others moves you to do what you can to lessen their burden, then your compassion, like His, has meaning. Your compassionate feelings translate into gifts you gladly give—heartfelt prayers, encouraging words, and practical help to those in need.

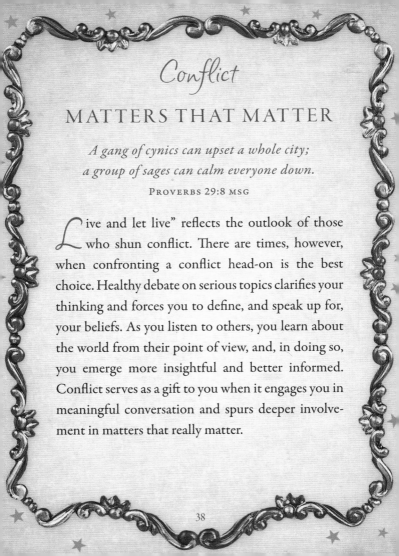

# Conflict

# MATTERS THAT MATTER

*A gang of cynics can upset a whole city;*
*a group of sages can calm everyone down.*

PROVERBS 29:8 MSG

"Live and let live" reflects the outlook of those who shun conflict. There are times, however, when confronting a conflict head-on is the best choice. Healthy debate on serious topics clarifies your thinking and forces you to define, and speak up for, your beliefs. As you listen to others, you learn about the world from their point of view, and, in doing so, you emerge more insightful and better informed. Conflict serves as a gift to you when it engages you in meaningful conversation and spurs deeper involvement in matters that really matter.

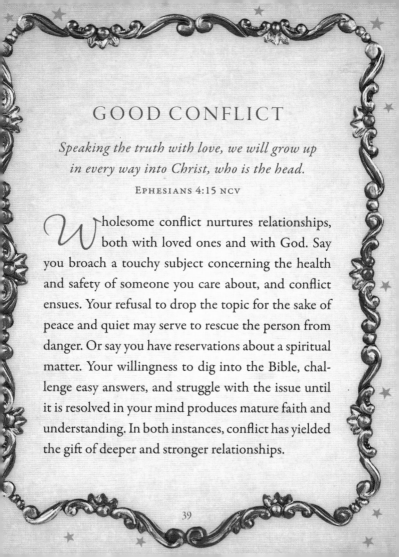

# GOOD CONFLICT

*Speaking the truth with love, we will grow up
in every way into Christ, who is the head.*

EPHESIANS 4:15 NCV

Wholesome conflict nurtures relationships, both with loved ones and with God. Say you broach a touchy subject concerning the health and safety of someone you care about, and conflict ensues. Your refusal to drop the topic for the sake of peace and quiet may serve to rescue the person from danger. Or say you have reservations about a spiritual matter. Your willingness to dig into the Bible, challenge easy answers, and struggle with the issue until it is resolved in your mind produces mature faith and understanding. In both instances, conflict has yielded the gift of deeper and stronger relationships.

# Conscience

## STEEPED IN HIS WILL

*We are confident that we have a good conscience,*
*in all things desiring to live honorably.*

HEBREWS 13:18 NKJV

If you wanted someone to lead you through a dense forest, you would want a guide with more than a basic idea of which direction to go. You would look for a guide who was informed, experienced, and thoroughly familiar with the territory! That is why a God-informed conscience, steeped in His wisdom and informed by His Spirit, is your best guide through life. Steeped in love for God and His commandments, your conscience is a gift that warns, guides, and directs needed change. Listen! It is possible that your conscience has been trying to tell you something lately.

# FIRST STEP

*"Believe me, I do my level best to keep
a clear conscience before God and my
neighbors in everything I do."*

ACTS 24:16 MSG

A guilty conscience is a gift. The discomfort of its nagging accusation night and day pushes us to admit that we have done wrong. It is what turns us to ask God for forgiveness, and what prompts us to put things right with the person we have harmed in any way. In addition, the next time we're tempted, our conscience reminds us what happened in the past, and we're warned against making the same mistake again. A guilty conscience is the first step on the path toward forgiveness and living with a clean, clear, and forgiven conscience.

# Contentment

## ENOUGH

*I have learned in whatever
situation I am to be content.*

PHILIPPIANS 4:11 ESV

The more we get, the more we want! Unchecked, our desires would keep us in a constant state of dissatisfaction, because there is always something vying for our possession—and our money. Yet when we put our trust in God to provide our real needs, our focus switches to what He has given and continues to give us. Our eyes turn to Him, and not to what we want or the things others possess. Our hearts fill with gratitude, whether we find ourselves rich or poor or someplace in between. The gift of contentment is the gift of always having enough.

# ON BEING YOU

*Each person should live as a believer in*
*whatever situation the Lord has assigned*
*to them, just as God has called them.*

1 CORINTHIANS 7:17 NIV

Are you content with the person you are? If you can say "yes," you possess a rare gift. It doesn't mean that you intend to never change, grow, or advance in your life, but it does indicate that you accept and respect yourself. You honor God, your Creator, by knowing you are no less in His eyes than anyone else, regardless of your appearance, abilities, challenges, or circumstances. Even more, you realize that He has a plan and purpose for you—one it would be impossible to carry out unless you are exactly who you are.

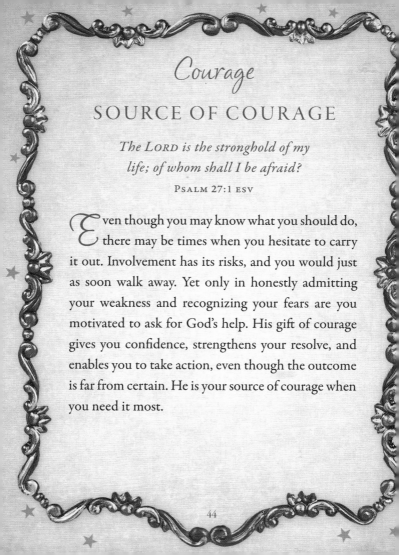

# Courage

## SOURCE OF COURAGE

*The LORD is the stronghold of my
life; of whom shall I be afraid?*

PSALM 27:1 ESV

Even though you may know what you should do, there may be times when you hesitate to carry it out. Involvement has its risks, and you would just as soon walk away. Yet only in honestly admitting your weakness and recognizing your fears are you motivated to ask for God's help. His gift of courage gives you confidence, strengthens your resolve, and enables you to take action, even though the outcome is far from certain. He is your source of courage when you need it most.

# COURAGE FOR THE DAY

*Be strong in the LORD and in
the strength of his might.*

EPHESIANS 6:10 ESV

One courageous effort isn't enough sometimes. Through periods of serious illness, persistent problems, or family difficulties, we feel we need a fresh dose of courage just to get up in the morning! That is exactly the gift God can give. Each day, ask Him for the courage you need to face the challenges in front of you. Open your heart and mind to receive both the courage to fight hard and the courage to retreat peacefully. Armed with His wisdom and strength, you will know the difference. Then get up and face the day!

# Daily Walk

## WALK HIS WAY

*"Come, follow Me."*

LUKE 18:22 NKJV

*Y*our daily walk, no matter where the path takes you, is a gift to you from the hand of your gracious God. As you travel the way He has laid out for you, you experience the joy and satisfaction of freely following His will. Even when you wander, you experience the comfort of being brought back to Him and realizing again the depth of His infinite love for you. Your daily walk is your always-unfolding, ever-revealing revelation of who you are and who He is. Walk with Him! Walk with joy!

# A REAL GIFT

*Everything you do or say should be done to*
*obey Jesus your Lord. And in all you do,*
*give thanks to God the Father through Jesus.*

COLOSSIANS 3:17 NCV

Without the circumstances and events of your daily walk, you would have no way of making God's will for you a reality. In the most ordinary events as in the most dramatic happenings, you have the chance to apply what you know about God in your thoughts, responses, and reactions. God's gift to you—your daily walk—provides you the privilege of bringing His love to the people you meet and of applying His heavenly purpose to your earthly surroundings. In your heart, in your hands, you have the gift you need to make it real!

# Decisions

## FREE TO DECIDE

*"So let us discern for ourselves what is right;*
*let us learn together what is good."*

JOB 34:4 NLT

When you come to a crossroads in life, it isn't always easy to make a decision about what to do. Perhaps both directions offer unique opportunities and challenges, and you can imagine yourself going either way. Even more, you don't sense any signs from God giving you guidance. Clearly, you're free to choose. Whatever you decide, commit your direction to Him, knowing He is right beside you. The decision you made, you may realize later, is the gift He had in mind for you all along!

# GO FOR IT!

*You ought to say, "If it is the Lord's will,*
*we will live and do this or that."*

JAMES 4:15 NIV

After a period of prayer, planning, and consideration, you've made your decision. You've weighed options, gathered information, asked advice, and acquired the resources and know-how you need to proceed. So go for it! Your earned confidence and levelheaded optimism propels you on the road to success, yet with one thing still remaining: God's good will for you. Along with your decision, a humble acceptance of His will keeps confidence from becoming arrogance, and allows every decision you make to stand as a gift of God to you.

# Desires

## ALL THE BEST

*For great is your love, reaching to the heavens;*
*your faithfulness reaches to the skies.*

PSALM 57:10 NIV

Those who love you want only the best for you. So does God, who loves you far more than even the most devoted person possibly could. Your heavenly Father desires to pour on you the gifts of His Spirit—love, joy, peace. He longs to shower you with the gifts of spiritual wisdom and understanding. He yearns to bring you gift upon gift that will enable you to gladly follow the path He has laid out for you. He desires only the best for you, and He has only the best for you.

# WHEN "NO" IS A GIFT

*These things happened as examples for us, to stop us from wanting evil things as those people did.*

1 CORINTHIANS 10:6 NCV

Sometimes what you pray for and don't get proves the best of gifts! Later you look back with relief and gratitude, realizing that what you had so fervently desired in the past would have made impossible the life that you now enjoy. Your insight tempers your present and future wants, provides the spiritual maturity you need to request good things, and leads you to wholesome and godly desires for yourself and your loved ones. Most importantly, you're reminded that, in God's hands, today's "no" is paving the way for tomorrow's resounding "yes."

# Discipline

## FOR A PURPOSE

*"The people I love, I call to account—prod and correct and guide so that they'll live at their best."*

REVELATION 3:19 MSG

Caring parents know the value of measured and appropriate discipline. Without it, children reach adulthood lacking the skills they need to lead a happy and rewarding life. Similarly, our heavenly Father disciplines all His children, regardless of age or status in the world. Its purpose is to nurture spiritual maturity, teach priorities, and enable you to live a life of joyful service and fulfilling accomplishment. Like the best parent ever, He cares about you, and the gift of His discipline is always timely, proper, and for your ultimate good.

# LESSON LEARNED

*At the time, discipline isn't much fun. . . .*
*Later, of course, it pays off handsomely,*
*for it's the well-trained who find themselves*
*mature in their relationship with God.*

HEBREWS 12:11 MSG

Perhaps it was an offended friend's hurt, a practical joke's unintended consequences, or a reckless venture's bad outcome. The moment we realized the pain our behavior caused, we vowed never to do or say such a thing again. Red-faced and feeling sheepish, we learned our lesson. In many ways, events discipline us so we can develop empathy and become less impulsive and more apt to think about the ramifications of our actions. Perhaps you remember a time that a lesson changed you for the better. Life's discipline is a gift that brings many other gifts in its wake!

# *Doubts*

## WITHOUT A DOUBT

*His delight is in the law of the LORD,*
*and on his law he meditates day and night.*

**PSALM 1:2 ESV**

Many well-meaning Christians hide their doubts, fearing that others would find their questions foolish or question their faith. Yet doubts, accepted as a gift, motivate believers to open the Bible and delve more deeply into its teachings, assertions, and promises. When you prayerfully consider what God says in scripture, His Spirit works in your soul to strengthen your faith, sharpen your knowledge, and open your heart to a fuller and more vibrant relationship with Jesus Christ. Maybe you won't find a clear answer to all your questions, but without a doubt you will increase in spiritual wisdom!

# LEAP OF FAITH

*"Lord, I believe; help my unbelief!"*

MARK 9:24 NKJV

As long as we remain in this world, we will ask questions that the Bible doesn't answer. For even the most committed believers, doubts will continue to nip at the edges of confidence and threaten the certainty of faith. The presence of doubt forces us to confront the gap between limited human intelligence and infinite divine wisdom. Are you letting doubt stifle your spiritual growth because you prefer your own understanding to God's purpose? Or are you letting each doubt work as a gift that compels you to take another leap of faith to God?

# Dreams

## GOD-POWERED DREAM

*"No chance at all if you think you can
pull it off by yourself. Every chance in
the world if you let God do it."*

MARK 10:27 MSG

From ancient times, the ability of the human mind to imagine what life could be like has spurred countless inventions and achievements. Dreams of something beyond today's reality remain dreams unless God-powered work follows. When your dreams for your future motivate you to set challenging, yet achievable goals, and begin a practical and realistic course of action, your dreams are God's gifts to you. Each one is His way of opening to you a bigger, better, and more fulfilling life—infinitely more than you could ever imagine.

# FROM HERE TO THERE

*Be transformed by the renewing of your mind, that you may prove what is that good and acceptable and perfect will of God.*

ROMANS 12:2 NKJV

Sometimes you have a dream, and you do everything you can to make it come true. But after years of trying, you find that things aren't working out the way you had hoped. What seems a cause for despair, however, might be God trying to get your attention! While your dream for yourself has brought you this far, the gift of God's dream for you is the one that will take you further. He alone knows the way ahead. Dream with Him, and watch your dreams come true.

# Emotions

## A FREE SPIRIT

*Refresh my heart in Christ.*
PHILEMON 1:20 NCV

Emotions are powerful. That's why controlling your emotions doesn't limit you, but frees you to pursue lasting goals and enjoy life's pleasures as God intended. Controlled, your emotions keep you from acting hastily, behaving inappropriately, and chasing after temporary highs. Self-restraint allows your emotions—love, compassion, happiness, even anger and sorrow—to serve you as God's gifts, and as an integral part of what it means to be alive. Regulated emotions enable you to respond to the world with heart, mind, and soul. When you capture your emotions, you're truly a free spirit!

# BEEN THERE

*Rejoice with those who rejoice,*
*weep with those who weep.*

ROMANS 12:15 ESV

Joy, sadness, sorrow, anger, peace—these are emotions that, if we're engaged with life, we experience throughout life. At these times, we appreciate those around us who understand our feelings and respond to us in a meaningful way. We remember the comforting touch of a friend who sympathizes with our loss. We still smile to recall the friends who were there to celebrate a milestone moment. Your emotions are God's gifts to you, and they're also gifts you bring to others. Why? Because you understand how they feel. You've been there!

# *Encouragement*

## KEEP GOING

*I press on to reach the end of the race and
receive the heavenly prize for which God,
through Christ Jesus, is calling us.*

PHILIPPIANS 3:14 NLT

Few of us can claim that we have never been
tempted to give up when the going gets tough.
Then along comes a friend, teacher, or mentor with
the words that restore our determination to go on.
Spiritually, the going can get tough—really tough.
That's why God reassures you with promises of His
presence, His strength, and His help. Repeatedly in
scripture, God refreshes you with the gift of His encouraging words. His Spirit works in you to renew
your strength so you can continue in His love until
the end. What is His message today? Keep going!

# TOGETHER

*Encourage one another and build one
another up, just as you are doing.*
1 THESSALONIANS 5:11 ESV

Most often, encouragement comes in words, but it is especially meaningful when it expresses itself with actions. Real and practical ways you encourage others in their daily walk—listening, advising, guiding, helping, and sometimes just being there—give your words weight and power. The person you encourage with the gift of your time and effort will never forget you! It's the difference between hearing someone say, "You can do it," and seeing someone step right alongside you, roll up her shirtsleeves, and say, "We can do it together!"

# Endings

## LETTING GO, GOING FORWARD

*"A grain of wheat must fall to the ground and die to make many seeds. But if it never dies, it remains only a single seed."*

JOHN 12:24 NCV

Endings can be difficult. When a loved one passes, a relationship fades, or our prospects dampen, we look back longingly to what used to be—the gifts we once enjoyed. Yet the gift of endings rests in what lies ahead. There's the cry of a newborn, the sight of young love, and renewed expectations as the horizon brightens with a new day. Your endings, though painful, are the gifts that train you how to lovingly let go of yesterday, confidently look forward to tomorrow, and unhesitatingly lean on God for strength and purpose.

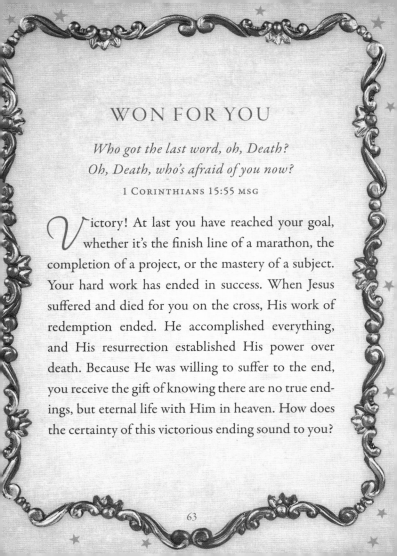

# WON FOR YOU

*Who got the last word, oh, Death?*
*Oh, Death, who's afraid of you now?*
1 CORINTHIANS 15:55 MSG

Victory! At last you have reached your goal, whether it's the finish line of a marathon, the completion of a project, or the mastery of a subject. Your hard work has ended in success. When Jesus suffered and died for you on the cross, His work of redemption ended. He accomplished everything, and His resurrection established His power over death. Because He was willing to suffer to the end, you receive the gift of knowing there are no true endings, but eternal life with Him in heaven. How does the certainty of this victorious ending sound to you?

# Enthusiasm

## FULLY PRESENT

*Live in his presence in holy reverence, follow the
road he sets out for you, love him, serve God,
your God, with everything you have in you.*

DEUTERONOMY 10:12 MSG

We know when someone is with us in body,
but not in spirit. Perhaps lost in thought,
distracted by anxiety, or simply inattentive, our visitor's lack of enthusiasm dismays us and even diminishes the relationship. In the same way, our lack of
enthusiasm for prayer, meditation, worship, and reflection on biblical truths weakens our relationship
with God. He speaks, but we're only half listening.
He blesses, but we hardly notice. If you know what
it's like, pray for the gift of enthusiasm, and then
bring it along on your next visit with God.

# NOW IS THE TIME

*Whatever you do, work at it with all your heart, as working for the Lord.*

**COLOSSIANS 3:23 NIV**

*H*ave you ever known someone who brings positive energy and excitement to even the most ordinary situations? Somehow things go better when they're around; you feel appreciated, happier, and more alive, and so does everyone else. Chances are that person is enthusiastic about the business of living! God offers to you the gift of enthusiasm. It comes with an optimistic outlook and a willingness to give of yourself—your full self—to whatever you're doing, wherever you are. Today is the day! If not now, when?

# *Example*

## REAL-LIFE EXAMPLE

*"If I then, your Lord and Teacher,
have washed your feet, you also ought
to wash one another's feet."*

JOHN 13:14 NKJV

When you want someone to truly get what you mean, you might cite an example. That way, there is less chance of a misunderstanding, because you've offered a clear, real-life instance. In the same way, Jesus, throughout His ministry among people, provided example after example of how we are to treat one another. He had compassion on people, He was kind to them, He healed them, and He forgave them. For us, there could be no misunderstanding! During His life on earth, Jesus left each of us a down-to-earth example for us to follow today.

# LIVE THE GIFT

*You should imitate me,*
*just as I imitate Christ.*
1 Corinthians 11:1 nlt

Your everyday example of kindness, gentleness, patience, and thoughtfulness is like a pebble tossed in the middle of a wide pond. Those touched by the warmth of your love pass it on to the people they meet. From there, goodness spreads, further and further out. Who knows whose day was made brighter or whose troubled soul found hope, by someone inspired by what you did? You may never hear about it, but on the far edge of the shore, someone experienced the refreshing waters of love. It happened because you gave the gift of a good example today.

# Expectations

## GIFTED EXPECTATIONS

*To the pure, all things are pure.*

TITUS 1:15 ESV

What you expect doesn't control what happens to you, but it does control how you see your circumstances. An attitude rooted in positive expectations and a willingness to highlight the good shields you from despair, even in challenging situations. When you expect to successfully solve your problems and meet your goals, chances are that you will. When you walk into a room expecting people to respond warmly to you, in all likelihood that is exactly what they will do. Why? Because your optimistic outlook is a gift, and they are hoping it might rub off on them!

# MUCH MORE

*"From everyone who has been given much, much will be demanded. And from the one trusted with much, much more will be expected."*

LUKE 12:48 NCV

No matter how little you may possess, God has given you a lot of something. Okay, maybe not money, but perhaps a heart for the needs of others. Perhaps a God-given spirit of joy, so needed by those burdened with sadness; or a well-learned lesson in the school of hard knocks, vital to someone who is now where you used to be. You have much, and the gift is this: you have the God-given privilege of sharing what He has given to you with those around you. You have more, much more, than someone you know today. The question is, who?

# Faith

## FAITH FOR SURE

*He breathed on them and said,*
*"Receive the Holy Spirit."*

JOHN 20:22 NCV

When you ask God for something you want, you are placing your request in His hands. Leaving it there, you wait for His answer. Maybe He gives it to you right away, or He may ask you to wait. He may even bless you with something much better, according to His good will. When you ask for the gift of faith, however, you've got it. Your heavenly Father delights in pouring out faith to all who ask with a believing heart. No need to wait before thanking Him for it—go ahead and thank Him now. You've got it!

# SIGHT OF THE HEART

*The fundamental fact of existence is that this*
*trust in God, this faith, is the firm foundation*
*under everything that makes life worth living.*
*It's our handle on what we can't see.*

HEBREWS 11:1 MSG

If you could see it, it wouldn't be faith. That's why those who look for physical signs will never find them. Why would it take faith to believe that the sky is blue or water is wet? Faith is more than what any human eye can perceive! Faith is God's way of inviting you to see things from His perspective, a heavenly perspective. It opens you to a fresh perception of what it means to live right here on earth. Faith is not a natural ability of the body, but a gift of God, received by His Spirit in your heart.

# Fear

## KEEP WOLVES AT BAY

*"Watch out for false prophets.*
*They come to you in sheep's clothing,*
*but inwardly they are ferocious wolves."*
MATTHEW 7:15 NIV

There are times when it's good to be afraid! Healthy fear keeps you from literally or figuratively stepping over the edge of a cliff. It compels you to shirk dangerous situations, and it makes you think twice before engaging in risky behavior. God's commandments—His warnings and guidelines—are intended to instill in you the gift of wholesome, life-preserving fear of what could harm you, physically, emotionally, or spiritually. His stay-away portions of scripture aren't your God crying wolf, but His gift to you. They're His way of clearly identifying the wolf.

# HEADS UP!

*God is our refuge and strength,*
*a very present help in trouble.*
*Therefore we will not fear.*

PSALM 46:1–2 NKJV

When you're afraid to live the life God is offering to you, it's time to focus on fear. Though He may prompt you to embrace new goals, unknown trials, or heightened experience, your natural hesitation does not need to keep you from these things. Instead, you can use your fear to give you a needed heads-up concerning the real-life challenges ahead, which in turn focuses your mind and heart on God, the source of your strength and courage. If you're afraid, receive your fear as a gift that invites God to walk with you on the road ahead.

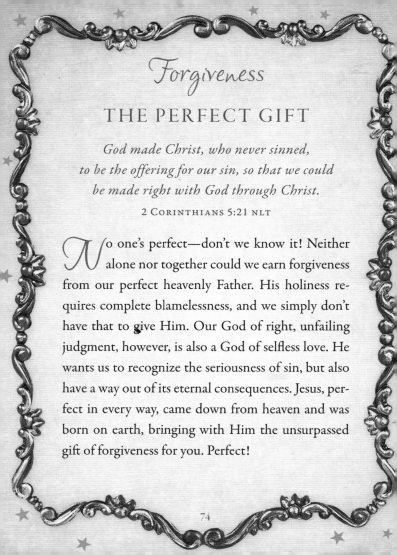

# Forgiveness

## THE PERFECT GIFT

*God made Christ, who never sinned,*
*to be the offering for our sin, so that we could*
*be made right with God through Christ.*

2 CORINTHIANS 5:21 NLT

No one's perfect—don't we know it! Neither alone nor together could we earn forgiveness from our perfect heavenly Father. His holiness requires complete blamelessness, and we simply don't have that to give Him. Our God of right, unfailing judgment, however, is also a God of selfless love. He wants us to recognize the seriousness of sin, but also have a way out of its eternal consequences. Jesus, perfect in every way, came down from heaven and was born on earth, bringing with Him the unsurpassed gift of forgiveness for you. Perfect!

# A GIFT FOR YOU

*Jesus said, "Father, forgive them,*
*for they know not what they do."*

LUKE 23:34 ESV

When the pain goes deep, forgiveness comes hard—yet forgiveness is the only balm with the power to heal the wound. Not even witnessing just and well-deserved punishment does as much to relieve the hurt inside as the willingness to genuinely and completely forgive your offender. Though your forgiveness may or may not mean anything to the one who has grievously wronged you, it will mean calmness, healing, and spiritual health to you. Yes, forgiveness is a gift you extend to others, but primarily it is a gift you are extending to yourself.

# Freedom

## PRICE OF FREEDOM

*God paid a high price for you,*
*so don't be enslaved by the world.*

1 Corinthians 7:23 NLT

On certain days throughout the year, we pause to honor those who have fought for our freedom. What a disgrace, however, if we were to invite on ourselves the very oppressions they gave of themselves—and sometimes their lives—to save us! Jesus died to gain an even more important freedom, freedom from the guilt of sin and its ultimate punishment. Though enticing temptations, old habits, and base desires continue to threaten, you are living now with the gift of freedom, because Jesus has fought for it, and He has won it for you. What's letting your freedom get away?

# SIGHT AND INSIGHT

*The Lord is the Spirit, and where the*
*Spirit of the Lord is, there is freedom.*

2 CORINTHIANS 3:17 NCV

The Holy Spirit develops and enhances your spiritual vision. In doing so, He frees you from faulty thinking and worldly distractions that distort your ability to discover God's truths and act according to His will. When you can see things as God sees them, you're able to go about your day with confidence and purpose. No longer are you held captive by indecision or left wondering whether you're on the right path. Your 20/20 spiritual sight and insight gives you the God-gifted freedom to live fully and joyfully every day. How is your vision? Ask God for a checkup.

# Friendship

## IT TAKES TWO

*"I've named you friends because I've let you in on everything I've heard from the Father."*

JOHN 15:15 MSG

Sometimes we're blessed with a friend we can confide in, rely on, and trust with our inmost thoughts. This friend, in turn, can depend on us to listen and to care. It takes mutual sharing and returned intimacy to make a friendship complete. Jesus, who calls you His friend, expresses His thoughts and desires to you. In the words of scripture, He tells you everything you need to know for your forgiveness, salvation, and peace with God. He offers to you the gift of His friendship, knowing that for a satisfying and fulfilling friendship, it takes two.

# CHOOSE CAREFULLY

*As iron sharpens iron,*
*so a friend sharpens a friend.*

PROVERBS 27:17 NLT

Parents worry if their teen starts going around with unsuitable friends. They're afraid the group's bad example will steer their son or daughter in the wrong direction. The influence of friends, however, doesn't stop when we grow to adulthood. Regardless of your age, your friends strongly influence your thinking and your decisions. What they do affects how you evaluate things; and where they go, you are apt to go, too. After all, you are friends! Just as your friendship is a gift to them, let their friendship be nothing less than a gift to you.

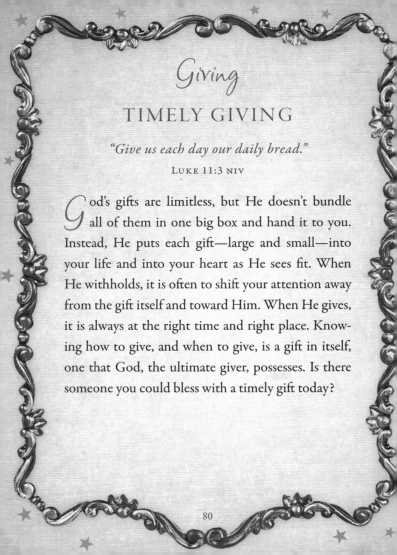

# Giving

## TIMELY GIVING

*"Give us each day our daily bread."*
LUKE 11:3 NIV

God's gifts are limitless, but He doesn't bundle all of them in one big box and hand it to you. Instead, He puts each gift—large and small—into your life and into your heart as He sees fit. When He withholds, it is often to shift your attention away from the gift itself and toward Him. When He gives, it is always at the right time and right place. Knowing how to give, and when to give, is a gift in itself, one that God, the ultimate giver, possesses. Is there someone you could bless with a timely gift today?

# WILLING TO GIVE

*See that you also excel in this grace of giving.*
2 CORINTHIANS 8:7 NIV

Some studies have shown that, in proportion to their earnings, many lower-income families give more to charities than their wealthier counterparts. Why? Perhaps they know firsthand what it's like to struggle simply to meet basic needs. Or maybe they give because they realize that the satisfaction of giving is a gift in itself, available to everyone, rich and poor alike. Your income doesn't determine your ability to give, but only the God-given gift of being able to willingly, joyfully, and generously open hands and heart to the needs of others.

# God's Will

## GOD'S GOOD WILL

*We know that God causes everything to work together for the good of those who love God and are called according to his purpose for them.*

ROMANS 8:28 NLT

After you have done everything within your power to set things right, you may find that your only option is to stand back and see what happens. Rather than worry while you wait, however, God offers to you this gift: trust in His will. By humbly accepting His authority over all life's circumstances, you gain the peace that comes with putting everything under control—His control. Sooner or later, you may glimpse His good purpose, but even if you don't, you still have the confidence of knowing that His will is being done for you and for those you love.

# FROM HIS HEART

*"I have loved you with an everlasting love;*
*I have drawn you with unfailing kindness."*

JEREMIAH 31:3 NIV

You may have heard someone say, "I think God is mad at me!" Things aren't going the way he or she would wish, and the comment, even made in jest, reveals an unfortunate view of God. In scripture, God reveals Himself as a God of care and compassion, goodness and mercy. Though certain behavior angers Him, and though He may correct you through the circumstances and challenges in your life, God's love for you never changes. From a heart of perfect, divine, and compassionate love, God's will for you is His gift to you.

# *Golden Rule*

## A GOLDEN GIFT

*"Do to others whatever you would like them
to do to you. This is the essence of all that
is taught in the law and the prophets."*

MATTHEW 7:12 NLT

The Golden Rule—treat others the way you want them to treat you—forms the foundation of healthy and wholesome interactions with others. The ancient adage invites you to put yourself in the other person's place and ask, "How would I like to be treated if I were in the same situation?" After you have your answer, you'll have what you need to build strong, positive, and lasting relationships. You'll know how to respond to those who don't follow the Golden Rule. Even acquaintances might notice there's something special about how you make them feel—important, respected, and loved.

# MOTIVATION MATTERS

*"How hard it is for those who have riches to enter the kingdom of God!"*

The Golden Rule comes with practical benefits. Some may practice it hoping to earn the admiration of others, make lucrative business connections, or garner goodwill so others will be indebted to them. Their desire for a rich reward—whether material or emotional—is neither a God-pleasing nor God-honoring motivation. With His gift of the Golden Rule to guide your relationships, God looks for your response of pure love as you strive to treat others the way He continues to treat you. The rewards of the friendship, gratitude, and appreciation of others are all God-given extras!

# Grace

## AIR OF GRACE

*By grace you have been saved through faith.*
*And this is not your own doing; it is*
*the gift of God, not a result of works,*
*so that no one may boast.*

**EPHESIANS 2:8–9 ESV**

You might compare God's grace to the air around you. You did nothing to choose or earn it, yet your physical life depends on it. Similarly, God's gift of grace is universal, available to all, and neither chosen nor earned by anyone. Just as air sustains physical life, God's grace sustains spiritual life. Unlike air that no one can refuse and still live, however, some refuse the grace that nurtures and supports their spiritual life and certainty of heaven. Because of His grace, God invites you to breathe deeply the life-giving gift of His grace He offers to you today.

# TOO GOOD—BUT TRUE!

*If they could be made God's people by what they did, God's gift of grace would not really be a gift.*

ROMANS 11:6 NCV

I f it sounds too good to be true," you are often warned, "it probably is." You are sensibly suspicious of offers promising "free" gifts! For this reason, God's gift of grace might make you pause. You might look for hidden costs, but you will find none. You might wonder how you can pay for God's grace, but you don't have to; Jesus has already paid the price, completely and in full. You might ask, "Why me?" He would say, "Why not you?" Yes, God turns earthly wisdom on its head, because His gift of grace is His gift of love to you!

# Gratitude

## GIVE THANKS

*I will give thanks to the L*ORD *with my whole heart; I will recount all of your wonderful deeds.*

PSALM 9:1 ESV

If you were to write your memoir, you would certainly mention the people who touched your life in positive and meaningful ways. You would tell your readers what they said and did, and the good that resulted from their influence on you. As you wrote about those special people, you might pause to utter a word of thanks for them. Similarly, as you reflect on all God has done for you, thanksgiving fills your heart. Those happy "coincidences"? Those "chance" happenings that worked out so well for you? The hand of God has touched your life! Give thanks!

# IT TAKES A VILLAGE

*I thank my God every time I remember you.*

PHILIPPIANS 1:3 NIV

It is said that "it takes a village to raise a child," but when we have grown up, we still need that village. For material, emotional, and spiritual support, we rely on one another as we use our abilities, skills, and resources within the community. We encourage, influence, and inspire with the things we do and say, each of us enriched by the presence of others. Without the "village" around us, we could never experience shared laughter, good times together, and heartwarming friendship. Today, give special thanks to God for His gift of your unique, life-sustaining village.

# Growth

## DEEP ROOTS

*He shall be like a tree planted by the rivers*
*of water, that brings forth its fruit in its*
*season, whose leaf also shall not wither;*
*and whatever he does shall prosper.*

PSALM 1:3 NKJV

You don't need to be a master gardener to appreciate the beauty of strong, healthy trees and robust, vibrant plants. These are rooted in nutrient-rich soil, they radiate energy and well-being, and they will thrive for a long time to come. Healthy spiritual growth depends on good soil, too. When your faith and confidence are rooted in God's truths, you are able to withstand life's harsh storms and damaging winds. Nourished in the soil of His life-sustaining Word, you receive from the hand of your heavenly Master Gardener His gift of continued vigorous and vibrant spiritual growth.

# KEEP LEANING,
# KEEP LEARNING

*Like newborn babies, you must crave
pure spiritual milk so that you will
grow into a full experience of salvation.
Cry out for this nourishment.*

1 Peter 2:2 nlt

Lifelong learning has gained a foothold in our society. Most of us realize that we need to acquire new skills or brush up on old ones to keep enjoying life to the fullest. Spiritually, too, lifelong learning is crucial. As you delve deeper into God's Word, you keep growing in knowledge, wisdom, and understanding. Childhood perceptions give way to mature discernment in spiritual matters and deeper awareness of what it takes to follow Him. For the gift of spiritual growth, keep leaning on Him. Keep learning from Him each day.

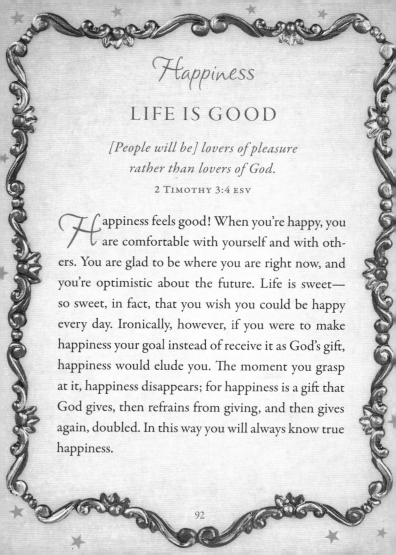

# Happiness

## LIFE IS GOOD

*[People will be] lovers of pleasure
rather than lovers of God.*

2 TIMOTHY 3:4 ESV

Happiness feels good! When you're happy, you are comfortable with yourself and with others. You are glad to be where you are right now, and you're optimistic about the future. Life is sweet—so sweet, in fact, that you wish you could be happy every day. Ironically, however, if you were to make happiness your goal instead of receive it as God's gift, happiness would elude you. The moment you grasp at it, happiness disappears; for happiness is a gift that God gives, then refrains from giving, and then gives again, doubled. In this way you will always know true happiness.

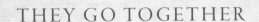

# THEY GO TOGETHER

*Whoever trusts the LORD will be happy.*

PROVERBS 16:20 NCV

Some argue that Christianity and happiness are mutually exclusive because of God's rules and regulations. Yet others say this: Christians are the only ones who have a real reason to be happy because of Jesus' life, death, and resurrection. Faith in God's willingness to love you, forgive you, and initiate a friendship with you releases you from doubt and despair. You have no need to try to please Him with great sacrifices or heroic deeds, but only a desire to respond to His commandments with humble obedience. Christianity and happiness? They are like two peas in a pod!

# Heart

## HEART OF LOVE

*God, make a fresh start in me.*
PSALM 51:10 MSG

We like to think of the heart as the residence of our inmost being. There we cloister our thoughts and secrets, carefully hidden from the eyes of others. Sometimes what is in the heart is so painful, so upsetting, that we close its door, allowing nothing to escape—and nothing to enter. God, however, stands at the door of every heart with the light of His love and compassion. He has the power to scatter the shadows, heal the wounds, and bring to your heart peace, comfort, and joy. Let Him transform your hurting heart into a heart of love.

# A NEW HEART

*"I will remove from them their heart of
stone and give them a heart of flesh."*

EZEKIEL 11:19 NIV

*P*erhaps you have known someone described as
an "old soul," or maybe those who know you
describe you this way. If so, they detect in you something that goes deeper than your experiences and the
knowledge you have gained in life. They see your
facility for discernment and understanding. It is
your possession of a heart able to generously extend love, warmth, and kindness to others; and to
graciously receive love, warmth, and kindness from
them. An "old soul" or the gift of a "new heart" from
God? He never fails to provide one to those who ask.

# Heaven

## QUESTIONS AND ANSWERS

*"God loved the world so much that he gave his
one and only Son, so that everyone who believes
in him will not perish but have eternal life."*

JOHN 3:16 NLT

With the question, "Where did we come from?" inevitably comes, "Where are we going?" Both queries have given philosophers ample grist for the opinion mill from ancient times to this day! Early on, however, God supplied the facts. You possess life because He desired to bless you with life and the ability to know Him and serve Him. He promises to grant you eternal life in heaven through your God-given faith in Jesus Christ. Now that you know about yesterday and tomorrow, let go of your questions and joyfully live His answers today!

# NOW AND WHEN

*"In My Father's house are many mansions;*
*if it were not so, I would have told you.*
*I go to prepare a place for you."*

Heaven is like money in a savings account. It isn't something you expect to need immediately, but you feel good knowing that it is there. God's promise of heaven to those who believe in His Son, Jesus Christ, is designed to make you feel good, too. In His promise for your future, you find comfort and consolation when you face bereavement and loss today. It relieves your anxieties and provides certainty concerning what happens when physical life comes to an end. Like money in the bank, the gift of heaven is for now and for when you need it.

# Hope

## WELL-FOUNDED HOPE

*I am counting on the LORD; yes, I am counting on him. I have put my hope in his word.*

PSALM 130:5 NLT

There are special people in your life you can count on—family members, friends, ministers, physicians. In the past, they have been there when you needed them, so it's only natural that you believe they'll come through for you in the future. The hope you place in them lets you relax, knowing they won't let you down. God's gift of hope extends to Him, too. He has helped you in the past, and you have every reason to place your hope in Him for any future need. Your well-founded hope lets you rest easy in Him.

# SAVED BY FAITH

*We were saved, and we have this hope.*
*If we see what we are waiting for,*
*that is not really hope. People do not*
*hope for something they already have.*

ROMANS 8:24 NCV

Even believers, when asked if they are saved, often reply, "I hope so!" You have a better answer because Jesus Christ has given it to you. Like any good leader, Jesus wants you to know where you're headed. Since He is the only one who has been to heaven, to earth, and back to heaven again, He's qualified to talk about eternal life and where you'll spend it. He promises salvation through faith in Him, so you know you have a heavenly home. Because God made the promise, you can not only hope so, but know so!

# Humility

## TO YOUR CREDIT

*By the grace of God I am what I am,*
*and His grace toward me was not in vain.*

1 CORINTHIANS 15:10 NKJV

On the surface, self-esteem and humility are opposites. How can you possess both at the same time? Understood from a spiritual point of view, however, both are part of a healthy, wholesome, and God-honoring self-image. You can own your earned accomplishments and observable achievements with pleasure, but here's where humility comes in: you give God the credit, because He is the One who has showered on you the talents and abilities you possess, and has given you opportunities to use them. With your gift of thanksgiving to Him, comes the gift of humility from Him.

# PAY IT BACK

*Be humble, thinking of others as*
*better than yourselves.*
PHILIPPIANS 2:3 NLT

Some people crave compliments, and others do everything they can to deflect them. Some smile with self-satisfaction, but others squirm with discomfort. While those reactions are common, none is consistent with godly humility. A spirit of humility allows you to graciously thank those who praise you yet balance their words with a true knowledge of yourself as an instrument in God's hand, merely doing what He has put in front of you do to. Encouraged by their kudos, however, you are reminded, too, how much a single compliment can mean. A returned compliment is even nicer than one received!

# Imagination

## A PICTURE OF GOD

*His names will be: Amazing Counselor,*
*Strong God, Eternal Father, Prince of Wholeness.*

ISAIAH 9:6 MSG

Have you ever sat back, closed your eyes, and imagined what God looks like? What He sounds like? Though it's impossible for the human mind to fully grasp God's being, He has given the gift of imagination. It is what the writers of scripture used when they, inspired by the Holy Spirit, conceived of word pictures to help convey God's appearance, the timbre of His voice, and the reality of His presence. He has been pictured as the Great Physician, Master Gardener, Mighty Warrior, Innocent Lamb, Heavenly Father, and Glorious King. How do you see Him? Use your imagination!

# COMING ATTRACTIONS

*Now I know in part; then I shall know*
*fully, even as I have been fully known.*

1 CORINTHIANS 13:12 ESV

Sometimes the imagination works like a newsreel going on in the mind. You might be watching yourself helping those whose needs have been on your heart lately. Or you're seeing yourself living a healthier lifestyle than you are now; enjoying a stronger, more vibrant relationship with the one you love; managing quite well at a higher job level; or reaching a goal you have always said you wanted to attain. With your imagination, you're looking at coming attractions. Now that you have the picture, you are ready to start moving it from reel to real!

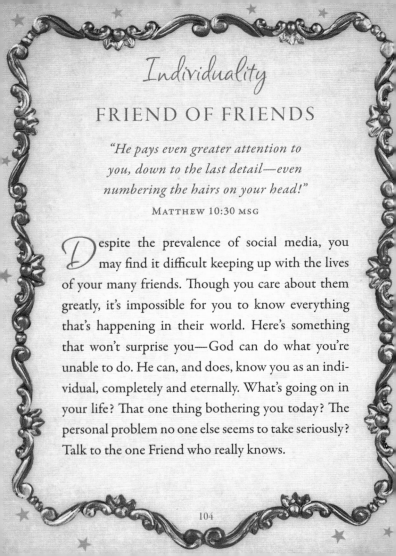

# Individuality

## FRIEND OF FRIENDS

*"He pays even greater attention to*
*you, down to the last detail—even*
*numbering the hairs on your head!"*

MATTHEW 10:30 MSG

Despite the prevalence of social media, you may find it difficult keeping up with the lives of your many friends. Though you care about them greatly, it's impossible for you to know everything that's happening in their world. Here's something that won't surprise you—God can do what you're unable to do. He can, and does, know you as an individual, completely and eternally. What's going on in your life? That one thing bothering you today? The personal problem no one else seems to take seriously? Talk to the one Friend who really knows.

# THE KALEIDOSCOPE

*Each of you has your own gift from God;*
*one has this gift, another has that.*

1 CORINTHIANS 7:7 NIV

Look through a kaleidoscope, and you can't help but smile. As you turn the lens, tiny colored pixels shift to create and re-create a brilliant array of circles, stars, and diamonds. Likewise, as you work together with others, each of you lending your individual gifts to the whole, fascinating things happen. Part of the design would be missing without you, just as if you took out even one color from the kaleidoscope. You're not the same as others, but integral to what others can do. That's the beauty—and the gift—of your individuality.

# *Joy*

## LASTING JOY

*For you make me glad by your deeds, LORD;*
*I sing for joy at what your hands have done.*

PSALM 92:4 NIV

Joy comes from God. God the Father has created you, and He has compassion on what He has created. God the Son has opened His arms to you and for you on the cross for your salvation. God the Holy Spirit has brought faith into your heart and continues to feed it, enabling you to love Him and extend His love to others through the things you do and say. Your straining for heavenly acceptance is over. No longer burdened with doubts about your relationship with God, you're ready to receive His gift of lasting, soul-deep joy.

# JOY IN THE WORLD

*I pray that the God who gives hope will fill you with much joy and peace while you trust in him.*

ROMANS 15:13 NCV

After weeks of gray, rainy days, you might despair of ever seeing the sun again! Above the clouds, however, the sun still shines—you know that, and so you're able to wait for the skies to clear. When adversity hangs over your life like a dark cloud, you might imagine that things could only go from bad to worse. Not so! Above these troubles, joy still shines, melting cares, bringing hope, and healing broken hearts. There is joy in the world, because joy, like the sun, is a gift of God—a warming gift that's waiting there for you.

# Kindness

## GIFT-GIVING OPPORTUNITIES

*Be kind to each other.*
EPHESIANS 4:32 NLT

Opportunities to perform great kindnesses come along once in a while. You witness an accident and stop to help, or dig into your savings to tide over an unemployed friend. More plentiful, however, are opportunities for little kindnesses, ones so small it is easy to miss them. For instance, you might hold the door open for the person behind you as you enter the supermarket. Remember to smile at the cashier as you pay for your purchases. Speak courteously to the clerk after a long wait. Wherever you see another face, there's an opportunity to give a little gift of kindness.

# FOUNTAIN OF KINDNESS

*Kind people do themselves a favor.*

PROVERBS 11:17 NCV

With God's gift of kindness, kindness becomes a way of life. Fewer sharp remarks drop from the lips; more occasions to assist, embrace, lift up, and encourage materialize where they were never noticed before. It's not all about what goes on outside of you. Your inner eyes perceive all the kindnesses God has extended to you, from the time you were brought into this world until this day. It is an awareness of God's benevolent presence that reaches to the core of your being, cleansing your heart, mind, and soul in a fountain overflowing with kindness. Consider His kindnesses today!

# Laughter

## FROM HEAVEN TO HERE

*A merry heart does good, like medicine.*

PROVERBS 17:22 NKJV

Here's a fun-to-practice health tip: laugh! It relaxes your body and mind, brightens your mood, and puts a proportion-providing light touch to heavy topics. The gift of kindly and uplifting laughter is your God-given way to add perspective when circumstances threaten to overwhelm you. The ability to laugh at yourself rightsizes your ego and keeps you grounded in reality; and to laugh with others strengthens bonds, builds friendships, and makes the happiest memories. It isn't hard to imagine that the lilt of healthy, wholesome laughter echoes throughout the halls of heaven!

# A SHARABLE GIFT

*Let there be no filthiness nor foolish talk*
*nor crude joking, which are out of place,*
*but instead let there be thanksgiving.*

EPHESIANS 5:4 ESV

When something makes us laugh, the first thing we'll do is share it with a friend. From the cartoons we find clever to the quips we deem quotable, humor reveals (subtly or not-so-subtly) our attitude, perspective, and maturity. Indeed, we display our character when we laugh! God-given laughter radiates kindness and promotes respect. It comes from a heart infused with love and compassion, and from a humble view of itself and a desire to lighten the burdens of others. It is clean and decent. It's a gift that blesses, a gift you will want to share with your friends.

# Life

## YOUR BUCKET LIST

*Teach us to realize the brevity of life,
so that we may grow in wisdom.*

PSALM 90:12 NLT

Have you made your bucket list? Many people compile a list of places they would like to see or things they want to do before they reach life's end. Taken with a lighthearted attitude, a bucket list stands as a healthy recognition that earthly life isn't a gift that you or anyone keeps forever. Rather, God graciously lends it to you for a span of time—time for you to go where He leads you and do everything He has planned for you. Why not create a bucket list? Never forget to live your precious life every day.

# FOREVER LIFE

*God has sent His only begotten Son into the
world, that we might live through Him.*

1 JOHN 4:9 NKJV

While the gift of physical life is temporary, the gift of spiritual life is eternal. You enjoy it now as faith blossoms in your heart and God's love flowers in your words and actions. When your years come to an end, eternity with God spreads before you, rooted in the truths He once planted, nurtured, and preserved in you. Spiritual life informs and enriches your physical life, as the fragrance of a rose enhances its beauty. You are more than what any human eye can see, because you possess life beyond forever.

# Light

## LAMPLIGHT

*God is light, and there is no
darkness in him at all.*

1 JOHN 1:5 NLT

When you snap on a lamp in a dark room, shadows vanish and darkness disappears. There is no need to sweep swaths of gloom under the rug, or push tiny particles of night out the door. The light did all the work for you. God's gift to you, the light of His Spirit and the shining star of His Word, has the power to dispel the darkness of grief and hopelessness. It is effective against the shades of guilt, shame, and despair. Like a lamp, God's light shatters whatever comes between you and a sunny, bright, vibrant, and joyful relationship with Him.

# SHINE ON!

*"You are the light of the world. A town
built on a hill cannot be hidden."*

MATTHEW 5:14 NIV

Jesus, born in Bethlehem, came to earth for a reason. His birth fulfilled God's promise to send a Savior—someone who could shine the light of God's love on you and show you how to reflect it. From the way Jesus spoke and acted, you know that your heavenly Father loves you and desires to heal you and draw close to you. Also, you see how He would want you to respond to others in your everyday life. He has brought His light to you. Now it is your turn to shine His light for others to see—and follow.

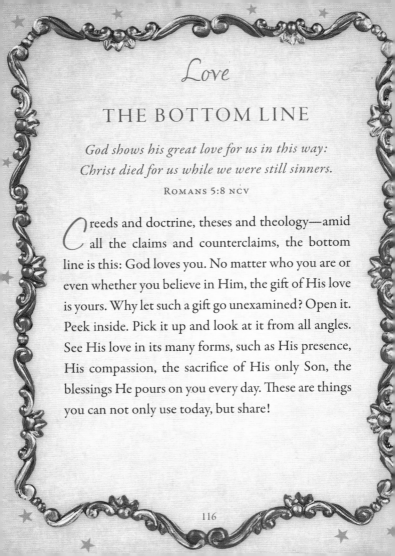

# *Love*

# THE BOTTOM LINE

*God shows his great love for us in this way:*
*Christ died for us while we were still sinners.*

ROMANS 5:8 NCV

Creeds and doctrine, theses and theology—amid all the claims and counterclaims, the bottom line is this: God loves you. No matter who you are or even whether you believe in Him, the gift of His love is yours. Why let such a gift go unexamined? Open it. Peek inside. Pick it up and look at it from all angles. See His love in its many forms, such as His presence, His compassion, the sacrifice of His only Son, the blessings He pours on you every day. These are things you can not only use today, but share!

# TRULY PRICELESS

*Give to the LORD the glory he deserves!*
*Bring your offering and come into his courts.*

PSALM 96:8 NLT

Have you ever tried to buy a gift for someone who has everything? In some cases, you might decide on a handcrafted or homemade gift as a token of your love for the person. Now imagine choosing a gift that expresses your love for God, who not only has everything, He made everything! What He asks is this: Respond to His love by sharing it with others. In the things you do and say, how you think, act, and speak, reflect His compassion and patience, His goodness and kindness, His love. Give the gift that money can never buy.

# *Mindfulness*

## PAY ATTENTION!

*So, whether you eat or drink, or whatever*
*you do, do all to the glory of God.*
1 Corinthians 10:31 esv

Paying attention isn't always easy, is it? When you are in familiar surroundings and going about your daily routine, your mind starts wandering, perhaps to tonight's menu, or to next summer's vacation. The gift of mindfulness—of being present in the moment—comes with practice. Start by giving your full attention to whatever you are doing for five minutes, then ten minutes. Gently rein in your thoughts as they start to stray. Notice the textures, colors, voices, and fragrances around you. Mindfulness awakens your spirit to vibrant, authentic life!

# ATTENTIVE LISTENING

*Now the Lord came and stood and called as at other times, "Samuel! Samuel!" And Samuel answered, "Speak, for Your servant hears."*

1 SAMUEL 3:10 NKJV

God's direction can come to you as advice from someone you trust; opportunities that open for you; clues He puts in your path; awareness of your responsibilities; knowledge of His guidelines. To make it possible for you to pick up on His direction, however, He offers to you the gift of mindfulness. Mindfulness keeps you alert to your present situation, your internal and external resources, and how you can best respond. He may desire your speaking or your silence, your action or your inaction, your risk-taking or your caution. Who knows? You will know, mindfully.

# Mistakes

## COMPLETE FORGIVENESS

*As far as the east is from the west, so far has
He removed our transgressions from us.*

PSALM 103:12 NKJV

Perhaps you smile when you hear someone say that "mistakes have been made." The speaker admits that wrongdoing has occurred but takes no responsibility for it. The hollow admission falls far short of what promotes spiritual growth, personal maturity, and strong character. Because you know that God will forgive you, you can go to Him with any shortcoming, mistake, or weakness weighing on your heart. You can say, "I did it," laying your burden at His feet, accepting His words of consolation and comfort, and most importantly, leaving your sins behind as you go forward. He has forgiven you completely!

# SMOOTH ROADS

*"Be strong and brave.
Don't be afraid or discouraged."*

1 CHRONICLES 22:13 NCV

Sometimes you might get off to a rocky start. You say or do the wrong thing; feel embarrassed or ill at ease; fail to get it right on your first attempt. Yet mistakes are gifts, because they're precisely what give you the know-how, experience, and skills you need to succeed. They prompt you to change your behavior for the better, perhaps asking advice from someone who is already where you want to go. The last thing you want a mistake to do is make you not try again! A rocky start, though temporarily jarring, can lead to a smooth road ahead.

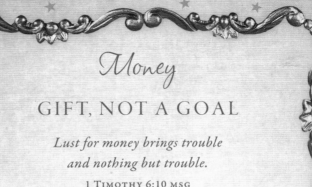

# Money

## GIFT, NOT A GOAL

*Lust for money brings trouble
and nothing but trouble.*

1 Timothy 6:10 msg

Money enables you to provide food, shelter, and clothing for yourself and those dependent on you. An adequate amount of money offers you choices, allows you comforts and entertainment, as well as educational and travel opportunities. Without question, money is a gift! When it becomes a goal, however, money becomes a problem. The desire to obtain more money clouds judgment. Reliance on its power to satisfy never fails to disappoint. Whether you have little or much, you must look to God for your sustenance and your happiness. Your goal isn't money, but to use it as God's good gift to you.

# SIMPLE MONEY

*"Seek first his kingdom and his righteousness,
and all these things will be given to you as well."*

MATTHEW 6:33 NIV

God has put a certain amount of money into your hands. You have stewardship over it and the freedom to spend, save, and share it as you see fit. Right away, you can see where potential problems lie! Spending gets out of control, leaving little to save and none to share. Or saving becomes an obsession, feeding fear of not having enough money; or sharing grows into a means to gain praise and admiration. Whew! That is why God makes it simple: put the Giver's priorities first and the rest of the gift will fall in all the right places.

# Needs

## YOUR WISH LIST

*"Everyone who asks receives, and the one who seeks finds, and to the one who knocks it will be opened."*

LUKE 11:10 ESV

*Y*ou have no doubt noticed that there is a difference between Santa Claus and God! Sure, you can hand either the red-suited jolly fellow or God your wish list, but only God has the power to provide you with everything you need. Your Father in heaven knows whether what you want today will serve you well tomorrow. He sees what would hinder and what will bless your spiritual well-being. Yet He invites you to present your list to Him now or anytime during the year. Why? Because each need, each want, is a gentle nudge to come before Him in heartfelt prayer.

# NEEDY GIFTS

*Let anyone who is thirsty come. Let anyone who desires drink freely from the water of life.*
REVELATION 22:17 NLT

When God fulfills your needs, you easily give thanks for His gift. It is not always easy, however, to see needs themselves as gifts. They are! Your spiritual needs draw you closer to God and turn your heart toward His Spirit's promptings. Your physical needs motivate you to use your talents and opportunities to meet them, and they awaken you to the needs of others. Only if you know what it is like to be without can you understand the joy of receiving. Yes, needs are gifts, intended by God to lead you to Him and to the God-honoring joy of sharing.

# Obedience

## GIFT OF YOU

*Do you think all God wants are
sacrifices—empty rituals just for show?
He wants you to listen to him!*

1 SAMUEL 15:22 MSG

Vou have heard the whine, "Do I have to?" When it comes to obeying God's guidelines, the answer is "No." God gave you free will to choose whether you will obey Him or follow your own counsel. When, prompted by His Spirit, you want to embrace His will for your life, you choose well. Your obedience stands as the finest worship you could offer, signaling to yourself and those around you that you put Him first not simply in theory, but in action. Though a gift of God to you, obedience becomes the gift of you to Him.

# BENEFITS OF OBEDIENCE

*The people who obey God's commands*
*live in God, and God lives in them.*

1 JOHN 3:24 NCV

Through your obedience, God showers countless blessings on you. When you put His commandments above human reasoning, you avoid many pitfalls and difficulties that wreck homes and derail lives. Obedience provides solid direction, builds strong character, earns a good reputation, and confers a healthy self-image. When sin tempts you, you pull back because you know better than to follow its course. Being obedient to God's time-honored truths, you inherit ancient wisdom that will serve you well today. Every opportunity you have to show obedience to God is God's good gift to you.

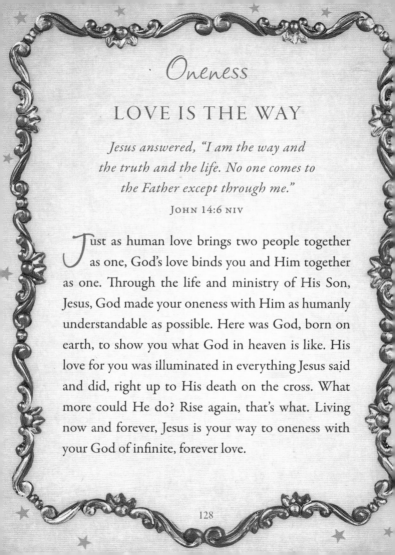

# Oneness

## LOVE IS THE WAY

*Jesus answered, "I am the way and the truth and the life. No one comes to the Father except through me."*

JOHN 14:6 NIV

Just as human love brings two people together as one, God's love binds you and Him together as one. Through the life and ministry of His Son, Jesus, God made your oneness with Him as humanly understandable as possible. Here was God, born on earth, to show you what God in heaven is like. His love for you was illuminated in everything Jesus said and did, right up to His death on the cross. What more could He do? Rise again, that's what. Living now and forever, Jesus is your way to oneness with your God of infinite, forever love.

# A COMMON BOND

*You are no longer strangers and foreigners,*
*but fellow citizens with the saints and*
*members of the household of God.*

EPHESIANS 2:19 NKJV

A reunion means remembrance, laughter, sharing, and celebrating a common bond. The bond—family, academic, military, heritage, or social—draws people together as one, knowing they can rely on one another for friendship, hospitality, and understanding. As a believer in Jesus Christ, you belong to the family of God. With all other believers in His life, death, and resurrection, you enjoy the forgiveness of sins through His sacrifice and have received the promise of reunion in heaven with Him and all believers. Oneness with family—your family—is your gift now and forever.

# Opportunities

## DAILY GIFTS

*"I tell you, open your eyes and look at the fields! They are ripe for harvest."*

JOHN 4:35 NIV

There is no need to wait for opportunities to come to you, because they are wherever you are and are yours for the taking. Your opportunity to grow spiritually, for instance, is there every time you sit down with God's Word and reflect on His presence in your life. Your opportunities for better health, stronger character, and financial well-being happen not as a one-time-only, out-of-the-blue chance, but build with each sound decision you make. There is nothing mysterious or magical about opportunity! It is a gift that is waiting for you every day.

# THE GRANDEST ONE

*This is the day the LORD has made;*
*we will rejoice and be glad in it.*
PSALM 118:24 NKJV

Like many of us, perhaps you look back and regret that you did not take a particular opportunity open to you at one time. Whether you were smart or mistaken to let that opportunity pass, however, the place you are today is where God brings more opportunities. Why look back? The gifts He has for you are in front of you, including an opportunity to lean on Him for support, direction, and guidance as you go forward on the path ahead. No matter what the past has been, you have the grandest of all opportunities right now—to follow Him!

# Past

## HE HAS HELPED

*He named it Ebenezer (which means*
*"the stone of help"), for he said, "Up to*
*this point the Lord has helped us!"*

1 SAMUEL 7:12 NLT

Why not take a few minutes to think about your life so far? For the blessings you have received, give thanks. For the dangers you have avoided; the tough times you have come through; the healing, growth, and wisdom that have brought you to this day, give thanks. The gift of your past serves to remind you of the many ways God has taken care of you, strengthened you, and nourished you. Each recollection gives you ample reason to believe He will continue to bless, guide, and protect you today and throughout every tomorrow.

# GOING FORWARD

*I said, "Let me remember my song in the night; let me meditate in my heart."*

PSALM 77:6 ESV

A balanced, objective look at the past offers insight into your strengths and weaknesses, aptitudes and difficulties. Wherever you see a pattern of bad outcomes, those past experiences can shed light on where your challenges lie, and then you can take steps to reverse the trend. Wherever you find personal satisfaction, achievement, growth, and passion, you are looking at the path God has laid out for you. Invite Him to help you use the gift of your past as you live and work today, and go toward the future, increasingly confident in your skills, knowledge, and abilities.

# Patience

## WHILE-U-WAIT

*I wait for the LORD to help me.*
PSALM 130:5 NCV

God is rarely early," someone once said, "and never late." God's gift of patience enables you to wait on Him, even though you don't know when He will act, or what He will do. You are not anxiously wringing your hands, or nervously pacing the room, because you have done what you have the power to do. Now the entire situation rests in His hands and your worries are laid at His feet. If this seems like a better way to meet life's challenges, pray for the gift of patience. Practice it, and take pleasure in His peace while you wait.

# A BETTER WAY

*Patience is better than pride.*

ECCLESIASTES 7:8 NIV

Are you more patient with others than with yourself? Just as others need your patience, so do you, especially when you fall short of your personal goals and expectations. Just as you would encourage someone else to try again, offer yourself encouragement. Affirm your best efforts, and give yourself time to learn and grow. No, change won't come in an instant, neither for you nor for anyone else. Perhaps that is what makes patience the prelude to real and lasting change. Give yourself the gift of patience, just as God is patient with you.

# Peace

## PEACE BEFORE PROOF

*Having been justified by faith, we have peace*
*with God through our Lord Jesus Christ.*

ROMANS 5:1 NKJV

The most intractable warfare happens not between groups or nations, but within an individual soul. At war with God, the soul requires reasons, answers, and explanations for pain and loss, destruction and death. It keeps up a futile fight for its own way, trampling the boundaries God has laid for the protection of those who love Him. The soul, consumed with anger, demands rights before reverence, proof before peace. Yet God stands, not to fight, but to forgive. He reaches out not with the sword of retribution, but with the gift of peace, the proof of His love.

# THE PEACEMAKER

*"You're blessed when you can show people how to cooperate instead of compete or fight. That's when you discover who you really are, and your place in God's family."*

MATTHEW 5:9 MSG

In any group, even among best friends, one wrong word, or a single unkind remark, can shatter peace. The bond of goodwill starts to fray, leading to increased tension, shortened tempers, and constant wariness. But while others pull away, one among them begins to mend the tattered ties, one thread at a time. First an apology, then listening, followed by understanding and healing, and finally a bond repaired, stronger and more resilient than before. Perhaps you are that one—the one who brings the gift of peace to your family, friends, neighbors, and community.

# Perfection

## PERFECTION MEETS PERFECTION

*"They will walk with me, dressed in*
*white, for they are worthy."*

**REVELATION 3:4 NIV**

God's perfection has been compared to a glass of pure water. If you add even a speck of dirt, however, the water becomes impure. The example helps us understand the gap between God's perfection and our imperfection, and why we cannot enter His presence as we are. God, in the person of Jesus Christ, won perfection for us through His death and resurrection. He bathes you in His purity, enabling you to approach God's presence at any time without fear. There's no longer a gap, but a meeting of holiness with holiness, perfection with perfection.

# PERFECT GIFTS

*Every good and perfect gift is from above.*

JAMES 1:17 NIV

With God, there are no one-size-fits-all gifts. Neither does He choose gifts for you that you don't need or can't use. They are never the wrong color, brand, or style. Will you open each one with wide-eyed eagerness? Maybe not. Though chosen with utmost care and sound purpose, some of the gifts He sends demand courage, commitment, and endurance—yet they are still good gifts, maybe even the most perfect gifts. Each one comes from the hand of your heavenly Father who is leading you on the path of perfection, gift by gift.

# Perseverance

## HE WON'T GIVE UP

*"While he was still a long way off, his father*
*saw him and was filled with compassion*
*for him; he ran to his son, threw his*
*arms around him and kissed him."*

LUKE 15:20 NIV

God is not one to give up. No matter how often we turn from Him, follow human reasoning, and chase our own desires, He comes looking for us. He sends His Spirit to stir our hearts, reminding us of where we belong and to whom we belong. He persists in His search through those who help us up, dust us off, and lead us back to the way of humility and holiness. Even though there may be times when you stumble, even fall, it is God who perseveres. How has His perseverance worked for you?

# CRITICAL COMPONENT

*What a gift life is to those who stay the course!*

JAMES 5:11 MSG

*I*f you possess the gift of perseverance, give thanks to God! Not everyone has the ability to stick to a project and see it to the finish. Not everyone dreams a dream and then does what it takes to make it come true. All of us need encouragement. Sometimes a friendly nudge is all it takes to boost our spirits, affirm our efforts, and make us willing to persevere. In spiritual pursuits, too, perseverance is critical. Maybe you could use a reminder today—or maybe there is someone you know whom you could bless with the gift of perseverance.

# Power

## FILL 'ER UP

*Power belongs to God.*

PSALM 62:11 NKJV

From faith flows power. Faith in God's love for you is the fuel that gives you the power to love others. The positive attitude that faith confers provides power to see beyond present troubles, to discover solutions, and to work for the common good. Because of your faith in God's power to forgive you and lift the burden of guilt from you, you possess the power to live freely and joyfully, unhampered by gloom or despair. It takes a full measure of spiritual power, and you have it, because along with faith, power is a gift of God.

# POWER FOR GOOD

*God's Way is not a matter of mere*
*talk; it's an empowered life.*
1 Corinthians 4:20 MSG

The question is not whether you possess power, but how you use the power you possess. Through God's Spirit at work within you, you have the power to bring God's love to those around you by being thoughtful, gentle, and kind. You have the power to help, listen, and care, and you know what a big difference those simple things can make to someone's day. Power isn't all about others, either. Within you, there's power to live peacefully, contentedly, and joyfully, even if the going is a little rough. You possess the power, so why not use it for good?

# Prayer

## YOU'RE INVITED

*"When they call on me, I will answer."*
PSALM 91:15 NLT

In another era, custom dictated that children did not speak to their elders unless spoken to first; neither servants their masters, nor commoners their king. What a reversal of roles God has set in place since ancient times! Your heavenly Father, sovereign Lord, and King of Kings, invites you to speak to Him anytime you want, and about anything that is on your mind. He encourages you to come to Him with praise, confession, gratitude, and all your requests. Even if you don't know what to say, He opens His arms and welcomes you into His presence. How about now?

# GOD'S PEOPLE PRAY

*"Where two or three are gathered in my name, there am I among them."*

MATTHEW 18:20 ESV

Private, solitary prayer nourishes soul and spirit. The time alone you spend with God puts you in touch with your inmost feelings; in the silence of your heart, you listen to His voice. But there is an equally edifying way to pray, and that is among others, with God in the midst of you. As you pray together, you hear the voices of those who express hopes, dreams, needs, and gratitude for His many blessings, just like you. Their words encourage you, and their presence reminds you of the fellowship you have with all God's people who pray.

# Presence

## HONORED HOST

*"Here I am! I stand at the door and knock. If you
hear my voice and open the door, I will come in."*

**REVELATION 3:20 NCV**

Think of a public figure you admire immensely.
Now imagine how you would feel if this person, at your invitation, were to come to your home.
Certainly you would be thrilled, and you are likely
to consider yourself honored and privileged that you
could offer hospitality to someone so important in
your eyes. How much more, then, are you honored
and privileged that God in heaven chooses to come
to you! The gift of His presence means that you are
never alone—never. Always, your most important
guest is as near to you as your heart.

# TAKE HIS HAND

*"Even to your old age and gray hairs I
am he, I am he who will sustain you."*

ISAIAH 46:4 NIV

When we are in the prime of life, we may believe we have no need of God. Then as we grow older and the illusion of self-sufficiency wanes, we tremble at the thought of illness, neediness, and loneliness. Where is God then? He is right beside you, where He has been every day of your life. Though youth, capabilities, faculties, and physical ability diminish over time, the gift of God's presence remains as strong, powerful, and vibrant as ever. As He reaches out for the infant's hand, the child's hand, the teen's hand, so He reaches out for your hand today.

# Problems

## STEP CLOSER

*In the day of my trouble I will call*
*upon You, for You will answer me.*

PSALM 86:7 NKJV

There's nothing like a big problem to precede a big step toward God! A major problem compels you to stop what you're doing and give it your full attention. When you realize that you can't handle it on our own, you are drawn to look beyond yourself to something bigger—to someone mightier. The comfort, assurance, and confidence that God provides strengthen your faith and affirm the trust you place in Him. There is no problem—big or small—that isn't a gift when it brings you closer to God.

# BE A SPORT

*"I will strengthen you and help you. I will hold you up with my victorious right hand."*

ISAIAH 41:10 NLT

In sports, a team does not know for sure how strong it is until challenged by another team. In a similar way, it is through the challenges you face in life that you learn how strong you really are. With nothing to test your strength, you would have no opportunity to increase problem-solving muscle, learn effective strategies for dealing with problems, and even how to lose a game without losing your will to try harder—and smarter—next time. Have a problem? Great! Win or lose, it is a gift when you give it your very best!

# Purpose

## THE COUNTED LIFE

*Aim at what is in heaven, where Christ
is sitting at the right hand of God.*

**COLOSSIANS 3:1 NCV**

In the family of God, everyone counts. There's no one born without purpose, and God's purpose becomes clear when you fix your eyes on Him. It's only then that you recognize yourself as a beloved child of God, born to love your heavenly Father, remain close to Him, and bring His care and compassion to others. His earthly purpose for you lies in the people who depend on you, the tasks and responsibilities He has put in front of you, and the godly pursuits that bring you genuine joy and fulfillment. Life counts, and so do you.

# PURPOSEFUL CHANGE

*Pursue righteousness, godliness,*
*faith, love, patience, gentleness.*

1 TIMOTHY 6:11 NKJV

When you embrace the gift of God's purpose for you, your life changes. No longer are you plagued with feelings of futility or emptiness. You see yourself as a person meant to live a godly life right where you are. Your particular circumstances take on depth and meaning as you explore the ways you can love, help, and serve people around you. Knowing your own purpose, your engagement and enthusiasm prompts others to find purpose in their own lives, as well. If you have any questions about your purpose, ask the One who gave it to you.

# Relationship

## BEYOND UNDERSTANDING

*The peace of God, which transcends all understanding, will guard your hearts and your minds in Christ Jesus.*

PHILIPPIANS 4:7 NIV

Who could comprehend your relationship with God? It is spiritual, for sure. His Spirit constantly prompts, directs, guides, and leads you to seek God and grow in awareness of His love. When you pray, read, and reflect on His message to you, your relationship deepens and strengthens. Yet your relationship is physical, too. It is visible in the way you act around others and in the things you say. It shows in your joyful attitude and generous nature. In addition, your relationship with Him is eternal! Who can understand it all? So you may as well sit back and rejoice in it!

# GODLY RELATIONSHIPS

*It is good and pleasant when God's
people live together in peace!*

**PSALM 133:1 NCV**

"No man is an island," wrote the poet John Donne as he reflected on our common humanity and reliance on one another. We depend on our community to supply our needs, while at the same time we contribute our particular talents and resources for the good of others. We thrive on healthy, wholesome bonds with those who mean the most, enabling us to give and receive love, our most unrelenting need for a full and happy life. Consider how your godly relationships enrich your life. Each one is a gift from God, who delights in His unending relationship with you.

# Renewal

## SHAKE IT UP

*He restores my soul.*

**PSALM 23:3 ESV**

When your time with God becomes routine, it is time for a shake-up! Ask yourself what would return grace, warmth, and sweetness to your meditation. A change of place could be as simple as moving from one room to another, or from inside to outside. You might add soft music or bring in a floral bouquet for beauty and fragrance. If you have a picture or object that draws your attention to God or His attributes, place it where you can see it and reflect upon its significance to you. Let Him renew and revitalize your spirit.

# REST, REVITALIZE, RESTORE

*Let the Spirit renew your*
*thoughts and attitudes.*

EPHESIANS 4:23 NLT

*D*oing the same things day after day makes you tired! Though you might not be able to spend a week relaxing at the beach, there are steps you can take to rest your body, revitalize your outlook, and restore your life's balance. How about a stroll through your neighborhood, a leisurely conversation with a friend, a time-out with a good book or movie, a visit to a local museum or historical site? God has put at hand ways for you to escape same old, same old. When you choose the one right for you, are choosing His gift of renewal.

# Respect

## GIVE AND TAKE

*"If I'm your Father, where's the honor?*
*If I'm your Master, where's the respect?"*
MALACHI 1:6 MSG

Respect is a gift everybody wants, but few are willing to give. Criticisms aimed at individuals in authority, as well as family members and friends, commonly lack validity, necessity, and goodwill. Even God does not escape! God, whose holiness, benevolence, and kingship demand utmost respect, often receives none. You have heard His name pop up in thoughtless expressions, strings of curses, and frivolous jokes. The gift of respect is a gift you deserve to receive from others, and a gift to give generously in thought, word, and action to others.

# EYES OF GOD

*If we live in the Spirit,*
*let us also walk in the Spirit.*
GALATIANS 5:25 NKJV

Imagine all the hurt we would avoid if we could but see God's Spirit reflected in the eyes of others! Then we would discover God within them. We would know each individual we meet as a brother or sister who is loved, forgiven, and accepted by God, same as ourselves. Respect would come naturally! But it doesn't. Respect remains a gift of God that He plants in the heart of those who recognize not only their own relationship with Him, but the relationship with Him enjoyed by others. It's a gift to use each time you look into the eyes of another person.

# Responsibilities

## THE RESPONSIBLE LIFE

*When I was a child, I spoke and thought
and reasoned as a child. But when I
grew up, I put away childish things.*

1 CORINTHIANS 13:11 NLT

As adults, most of us willingly take on our responsibilities. Whether centered on home or work, your responsibilities are the threads that weave you into your family group and social community. For example, you accept the responsibility of friendship by being a friend at all times, and the responsibility of following God by doing so every day. Responsibilities create the design of your character, and shape the pattern of your thoughts, words, and actions. Though responsibilities may seem burdensome or inconvenient at times, each one you have is a gift from the hand of your heavenly Father.

# BIG FAT GIFT

*"Every good tree bears good fruit."*
MATTHEW 7:17 NIV

God-given responsibilities are like big gift boxes that hold many, many little gifts inside. By gladly embracing your responsibilities, you find meaning and purpose in life—plus genuine joy. By committing yourself to your responsibilities, you gain integrity, patience, and endurance—plus earned self-esteem. By looking to others for help and advice in bearing your responsibilities, you get encouragement and know-how—plus friendship. By leaning on God for His presence, strength, and encouragement, you receive all those things—plus a living, tried-and-true faith. Responsibilities often come in a big fat box, but don't be afraid to open it!

# Savior

## ALL-SUFFICIENT GIFT

*The free gift of God is eternal life*
*through Christ Jesus our Lord.*
ROMANS 6:23 NLT

Many of us take pride in living as self-sufficient adults, able to fend for ourselves and our loved ones. Our pride, however, often makes us reluctant to ask for what we can't give ourselves, mainly a heart at peace with God. Jesus, God's Son, is the gift He sent into the world to be our Savior—that is, to take on our guilt and provide us with His purity. Don't let pride get in the way of asking for His forgiveness, but turn toward God's all-sufficient gift to you: Jesus, your Savior, the Prince of Peace.

# JESUS SAVES

*It is pleasing in the sight of God our Savior,*
*who desires all people to be saved and to*
*come to the knowledge of the truth.*

1 TIMOTHY 2:3–4 ESV

Jesus saves." You might see the simple message glowing from a lighted sign, scribbled in the margins of a book, or spray-painted across the bricks of an abandoned building. Yes, Jesus saves! He saves from guilt by inviting your admission of sin and your humble acceptance of His forgiveness. He saves to grant you an earthly life of joy and freedom, and He saves for the purpose of granting you eternal life in heaven. Jesus saves! The most important place you can ever find those words is impressed upon your heart.

# Security

## SECURITY THAT MATTERS

*Lead me to the rock that is higher than I.*

PSALM 61:2 NKJV

No matter how much money, time, and effort we devote toward protecting ourselves from outside perils, the security that matters lies inside the heart, where God dwells. God's security is real, because your confidence in His control keeps you from despair when outside defenses fail. His security is effective, because your faithfulness to His Word pulls you from sin when temptation threatens your godly way. His security is lasting, because no matter how many other shields shatter, your strength rests in Him, who is forever. How does the gift of His security matter to you?

# SECURE FRIENDSHIP

*Thank the LORD because he is good.*
*His love continues forever.*
PSALM 118:1 NCV

"Unfriending" someone isn't a modern phenomenon, unique to social media. Throughout the history of human relationships, friendships have unraveled, marriages have disintegrated, and loved ones have left broken hearts behind. The history of God's way with people, however, tells a different story. Though many "unfriend" Him to make friends with the world, His love for them remains unchanged. When others refuse His offer of a relationship with them, His love for them stays solid and secure. Through it all, His invitation to become His friend again still stands. You can rest secure in His love for you!

# Serenity

## IT WORKS!

*"God will help you deal with whatever hard things come up when the time comes."*

MATTHEW 6:34 MSG

Few of us would keep buying a product we find ineffective. Yet worry, stress, and anxiety are three popular "products" we keep using, even though we know they are useless. Worry never solves a problem, stress only makes it harder, and anxiety wears us out, physically and emotionally. So throw them out! Now you have space for God's gift of serenity, proven highly effective for calming your mind, clearing your vision, and resting your soul. There's more! Serenity says to God, "I can relax. You will see me through to the end."

# LIGHTEN UP

*"Come to me, all of you who are weary and carry heavy burdens, and I will give you rest."*

MATTHEW 11:28 NLT

Overwhelming to-do list? Tense relationships? A full-blown case of self-reproach? If you can relate to any of these feelings (or worse, all three!), it is time to lighten up. Lighten up on the number of times you say, "Yes, I'll do it." Decide to delegate it—or eliminate it. Lighten up on what you expect from others, what it takes to offend you, and how you respond. Learn to laugh. Lighten up on what you expect from yourself, because you are doing your best, and the rest is up to God. Take it easy, and embrace His gift of heart-deep serenity.

# Service

## SERVING THE SERVANTS

*When he had finished washing their feet,*
*he. . .returned to his place. "Do you understand*
*what I have done for you?" he asked them.*

JOHN 13:12 NIV

A wealthy householder might hire men and women to serve in the home as cooks, maids, and gardeners. In God's kingdom, however, the opposite holds true. Though Creator, King, and owner of all things, God serves you. He nourishes your thoughts with wisdom and understanding through His Word; He cleanses your soul from guilt and shame through the work of Jesus Christ; He lifts away what burdens you, and cultivates within you the sweet fragrance of faith, hope, and love. The gift of service is His to give. How may He serve you now?

# CLASS ACT

*"I've laid down a pattern for you.*
*What I've done, you do."*

JOHN 13:15 MSG

The best teachers don't simply talk: they demonstrate what they mean. Whether through actions, graphs, photos, displays, or illustrations, they do whatever they can so their students can understand and apply the information. Jesus, our premier Teacher, came down from heaven in human form so we could receive more than just words about God. Jesus exhibited what God is like in His love, mercy, and compassion for people. He showed what God does by forgiving, healing, and blessing. He did it all so you could understand what service is, and apply it to your life each day.

# Sharing

## THE GIFT OF YOU

*The godly are generous givers.*

PSALM 37:21 NLT

Perhaps you learned from an early age to share your toys. Now, as a grown-up, you know to share what you have been given with people in need. But there's something else you share that you might not be aware of, and that's you. Whenever you are around others, you are sharing your words and actions, mood and attitude, opinions and feelings. You are sharing the person you are through the expression on your face, the gestures you use, and the warmth of your responses to others. The God-given gift of sharing is yours. What "you" are you sharing today?

# PLENTY FOR YOU

*The one who blesses others
is abundantly blessed.*

PROVERBS 11:25 MSG

"What's in it for me?" sounds like a selfish question, but when it comes to sharing, the answer is, "Plenty!" Besides the good feeling of being able to help someone out, there is spiritual growth in contributing to the common good. Sharing proves your reliance on God to meet your needs, and frees you from fear of the future. It develops the God-pleasing habits of thoughtfulness, consideration for others, and bigheartedness; in addition, sharing is your opportunity to follow Jesus' example. While your willingness to share is God's gift to others, it is no less His gift to you.

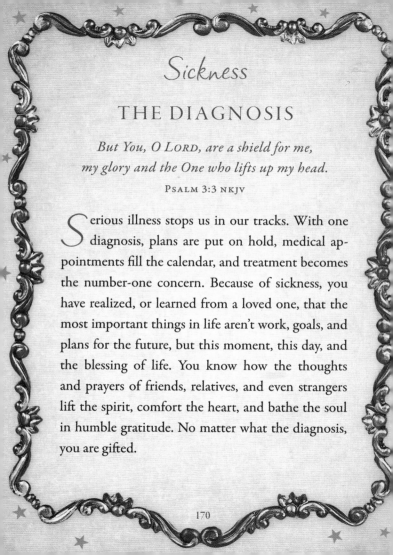

# Sickness

## THE DIAGNOSIS

*But You, O LORD, are a shield for me,*
*my glory and the One who lifts up my head.*
PSALM 3:3 NKJV

Serious illness stops us in our tracks. With one diagnosis, plans are put on hold, medical appointments fill the calendar, and treatment becomes the number-one concern. Because of sickness, you have realized, or learned from a loved one, that the most important things in life aren't work, goals, and plans for the future, but this moment, this day, and the blessing of life. You know how the thoughts and prayers of friends, relatives, and even strangers lift the spirit, comfort the heart, and bathe the soul in humble gratitude. No matter what the diagnosis, you are gifted.

# THE DOCTOR IS IN

*Jesus. . .said to them, "It is not the healthy people who need a doctor, but the sick. I did not come to invite good people but to invite sinners."*

MARK 2:17 NCV

How sound is the health of your soul? Your Great Physician, Jesus, has the power to enliven faith that has grown cold, calm feverish seeking of love that can find none, and heal the hurt of loneliness, loss, and hopelessness. He has the ability to soothe anxieties that tug at your heart, remove the burden of sadness, set your feet on the right path, and, most importantly, fix a broken relationship with your heavenly Father. For the stricken soul—for your soul—even a mild "achoo!" is a gift inviting you to pay Him a visit.

# Silence

## THE DESERT

*"Am I a God at hand, declares the*
*Lord, and not a God far away?"*
### JEREMIAH 23:23 ESV

I t may feel as if God is not there. You pray, but receive no answer—no warm assurance of His presence. No confidence that things will turn out okay. The holy ancients often referred to God's silence as a spiritual desert. Parching thirst, but no water. Blinding heat, but no shade. Nonetheless, they recognized His silence as a gift—a gift that tests commitment. A gift that says, "Will you stay with Me, even in My seeming absence?" You long for the sweetness of God's embrace! If you think it isn't there, will you stay in the desert?

# SHARING SILENCE

*The Lord will hear when I call to Him.*

PSALM 4:3 NKJV

In a casual chat between friends, silence can act as a portal to meaningful conversation. One person feels secure enough to divulge a long-held burden. Another senses the atmosphere right to confide a burden that has been on her heart for a long time. Silence between loved ones is necessary, for it is often through silence that we find an opening to talk about what is really important to us. That silence between you and God? Perhaps He's waiting for you to share with Him what lies within your heart of hearts.

# Simplicity

## CLEAR THE CLUTTER

*We set our eyes not on what we see but on what we cannot see. What we see will last only a short time, but what we cannot see will last forever.*

2 CORINTHIANS 4:18 NCV

Suppose you bought a piece of original art, and you wanted to display it in your home. To highlight the piece, you might clear a space for it by removing clutter and other distractions. Now, when your friends enter your home, their attention goes directly to the artwork. As God enters your heart, do you sense His presence? If not, perhaps other attractions are pulling your thoughts away from Him. Many things are vying for your attention, and you are unable to focus on your most treasured possession. Clear the clutter! Ask God for His gift of simplicity.

# SIMPLE SOLUTION

*I prayed to the LORD, and he answered
me. He freed me from all my fears.*

PSALM 34:4 NLT

A rule to remember when solving a problem is not to complicate it. When you can pinpoint the root of the problem, you are already halfway to a solution! If, in your walk with God, you are coming up against complications that limit your spiritual growth, it is time to determine the root problem. Allow God to strip away fears, excuses, opinions, and speculation, and reveal to you the core question that is tugging at your inmost heart. His gift of spiritual simplicity puts you only a prayer away from the solution.

# Smile

## SMILE ANYWAY

*A cheerful heart brings a smile to your face.*

PROVERBS 15:13 MSG

That rainy-day feeling—you just can't seem to shake it. Though you can't put your finger on anything that would bring on the clouds, you are not finding anything to smile about, either. Smile anyway! A smile on your face lifts your mood, scatters the shadows, and lets a few rays of sunshine into your heart. Almost without realizing it, you begin to feel better about yourself, and that goes right along with a positive attitude, an attractive disposition, and the ability to enjoy the God-given pleasures in life. No matter what the weather outside, that is something to smile about!

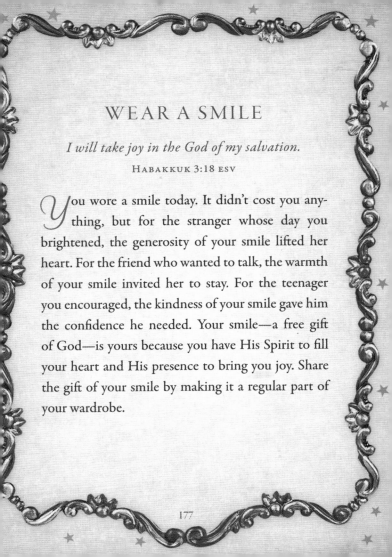

# WEAR A SMILE

*I will take joy in the God of my salvation.*
HABAKKUK 3:18 ESV

You wore a smile today. It didn't cost you anything, but for the stranger whose day you
brightened, the generosity of your smile lifted her
heart. For the friend who wanted to talk, the warmth
of your smile invited her to stay. For the teenager
you encouraged, the kindness of your smile gave him
the confidence he needed. Your smile—a free gift
of God—is yours because you have His Spirit to fill
your heart and His presence to bring you joy. Share
the gift of your smile by making it a regular part of
your wardrobe.

# Solitude

## THE BEST COMPANY

*Be still, and know that I am God.*
PSALM 46:10 NKJV

When you are with someone you love, you have no desire for anyone else's presence. Your beloved fills all your needs, and you bask in the compliment of the other's complete attention. It is not hard to imagine that God, who loves you beyond all measure, yearns for time alone with you—only you. How He must delight in your full concentration on His Word, and your deep desire to listen, hear, and reflect on His care for you. God's gift of solitude with Him puts you in the very best of company.

# GOOD SOLITUDE

*Test yourselves to make sure you are solid in the faith. Don't drift along taking everything for granted. Give yourselves regular checkups.*

2 CORINTHIANS 13:5 MSG

Just as sleep refreshes your body and mind, solitude nourishes your soul. Time alone in a quiet, peaceful environment lets you center your thoughts on your spiritual growth, your inmost values, and your relationship with God. It lends itself to self-examination, honest answers, and sincere repentance. Your solitude draws you into God's comfort, soothes you with His forgiveness, and revitalizes you with His assurance that He will always love you—always. Solitude is a gift that brings you back into the world more confident, stronger, and surer than ever of God's presence in your life.

# Strength

## NOT INFECTED

*Your enemy the devil prowls around like a*
*roaring lion looking for someone to devour.*

1 PETER 5:8 NIV

Few of us willingly take on foes stronger and more powerful than ourselves. How foolish, and quite possibly fatal. Yet we often think we can fight temptation on our own. Do we realize what we're up against? Satan is strong, powerful, and real, and his purpose is to disconnect you from God. On your own, you cannot overcome him. God, through the death and resurrection of Jesus, has won victory over sin. Though sin affects your life, sin need not infect the relationship you have with Him. Rely on the gift of His strength. How wise, and most certainly life-giving.

# STRENGTH BUILDER

*The LORD is my strength and my shield.*

PSALM 28:7 NKJV

It takes time to build strength, whether you plan to run a marathon, bike up a hill, swim across a lake, or walk with God. With practice, however, you're able to go a little further each day. The more time, energy, and attention you give, the more satisfaction you receive, along with increased skill and experience. Plus, strength. Your daily walk with God strengthens your faith, keeps your spirit in tune with His will, and gets your spiritual muscles in shape. It takes time, but God never fails when it comes to using His strength to make you strong.

# *Struggle*
## SUCCESSFUL STRUGGLES

*I am very happy to brag about my weaknesses.*
*Then Christ's power can live in me.*

2 CORINTHIANS 12:9 NCV

People undefeated by their struggles inspire us. They cope with their hardships successfully, even cheerfully, and we want to learn from them how to face our own struggles with such courage and optimism. We often find that they credit God for their ability to overcome, and their words affirm our faith and demonstrate God's vital, living power at work. Their struggles are a gift to us! In the same way, your struggles are gifts to you, able to increase experience and strengthen faith—and a gift to others when they see how successfully, even cheerfully, you handle them.

# ROADWORTHY FAITH

*"I will refine them like silver and*
*purify them like gold."*
ZECHARIAH 13:9 NLT

Think that your faith in God will smooth the path ahead? Think again! No human life is without struggles of some kind; they come to everyone, believer and nonbeliever alike. For the believer, however, physical, spiritual, and relationship struggles serve to test faith in real-life situations. Struggles, confronted with courage and perseverance, strengthen and refine faith, rendering it increasingly robust and roadworthy. God never promised to remove every bump, every pothole, every rough place—but He has promised to go with you every inch of the way.

# Success

## ASSURED SUCCESS

*"The LORD has already cleared the way for you."*
JUDGES 4:14 NCV

We love to celebrate success! When the goal has been reached, the reward obtained, the subject mastered, we have every reason to feel good about our efforts and the happy outcome. Some success, however, passes us by because we don't recognize it as success. Why? Because the outcome wasn't what we thought it would be and hoped it would be. Yet whenever God gives you the task—when His Spirit inspires you toward an objective—there will be a successful result. Don't be afraid to take it on, because He will give success.

# EVERYTHING YOU NEED

*"When my soul fainted within me,
I remembered the LORD."*

JONAH 2:7 NKJV

Long before we succeed at reaching a significant goal, we're often waylaid by feelings of inadequacy. Though we have made many good strides forward, we start wondering if we have what it takes to go further. Instead of looking to yourself with the question, however, look to God and what He says in scripture. Reflect on His promises of help, support, strength, and protection whenever you are following His will and purpose for your life. With His words in your mind, put Him to the test! Expect, and receive, everything you need to achieve God's gift of true success.

# *Tension*

## SOMETHING NOT OKAY?

*Those who are wise will find a time
and a way to do what is right.*

ECCLESIASTES 8:5 NLT

Your tension usually means that something isn't right. What is going on around you is out of sync with, or doesn't match what you think should be happening. The tension you feel is a gift when it compels you, not to avoid the issue, but to work toward resolution. The gift of outer tension between you and others motivates you to take the initiative, invite productive communication, and enjoy a renewed relationship. The gift of inner tension between you and your honest feelings urges you to listen more closely to yourself and to God. Feeling tense? Make it right.

# TENSION'S JOB

*Give me understanding that I may live.*
PSALM 119:144 ESV

When there is positive tension between you and what you want to achieve, welcome it! This is not debilitating stress, but a healthy tautness that keeps you intellectually alert, spiritually motivated, and physically energetic. It is the opposite of complacency that would have you looking at but never reaching toward; dreaming of but never stepping out. Good tension takes you out of your comfort zone—that is its job! Before you rush to get rid of it, ask first if your tension could be a healthy, God-given gift, intended to put some snap back into your life!

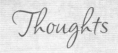

# *Thoughts*

## THINKING OF YOU

*For I know the thoughts that I think toward*
*you, says the LORD, thoughts of peace and*
*not of evil, to give you a future and a hope.*

JEREMIAH 29:11 NKJV

A penny for your thoughts." "Sure," replies your
gracious God. Throughout the pages of scripture, God reveals His thoughts toward you. His
words of love, compassion, and understanding reflect
His infinite love for you. His promise of forgiveness
no matter what the sorrowful heart confesses, and
His plan for your salvation through the work of Jesus Christ, prove His thoughts are not just for today,
but for eternity. Through the power of His Spirit, inspired writers made the gift of God's thoughts available to you, and you don't even need to give Him a
penny—just your prayerful attention.

# GOOD THOUGHT

*Fix your thoughts on Jesus, whom we acknowledge as our apostle and high priest.*

HEBREWS 3:1 NIV

Positive thoughts are like vitamins for the mind. They are mood boosters, and when you're feeling upbeat, you are better equipped to focus on what is working rather than despairing over what is not. When it is time to tackle what isn't working, an optimistic outlook gives you mental energy, along with a willingness to discover and implement practical solutions. If the gift of positive thinking doesn't come naturally to you, choose it for yourself. Write down three affirmative statements about your situation every morning. Remind yourself of them during the day. Soon, you'll be taking your daily "vitamins" almost without, well, thinking!

# Time

## OPEN NOW!

*"We must quickly carry out the tasks assigned us by the one who sent us. The night is coming, and then no one can work."*

JOHN 9:4 NLT

Thank God that's over!" you might announce after getting through a difficult time in your life. Of course, you experience wonderful times you wish could last forever! God gives the gift of time moment by moment. Now is the moment He offers for you to think, feel, act, dream, and imagine. He invites you to fill it up, shake it up, and use it up by immersing yourself in the present day with heart, soul, and mind. Unlike many of God's gifts, time doesn't last forever. So go ahead, and open the gift of now—now!

# WATCH FOR ROBBERS

*"Who of you by worrying can add
a single hour to your life?"*

LUKE 12:25 NIV

Two thieves lurk at your door, looking for ways to steal Today. The first thief's name is Yesterday, and Yesterday drags your thoughts back through past regrets, bygone affronts, and long-ago sufferings. The second thief's name is Tomorrow. Tomorrow suggests you worry about what might happen and imagine the disasters waiting for you right around the corner. All too often, the two thieves divide your day between them! God has given you the gift of Today. Ask Him to help you guard it and keep it, and spend His precious gift on nothing else but Today.

# Traditions

## FAMILY TRADITIONS

*God sets the solitary in families.*

PSALM 68:6 NKJV

Family traditions can be a rich source of solidarity, stability, and pride. Elder members offer perspective, experience, and wisdom to the younger; children discover their heritage, benefit from multigenerational relationships, and provide living proof that the family line continues. Christian traditions play a similar role. They connect you to what has proven helpful to the spiritual lives of past believers. You benefit from the presence of others who can encourage you in your walk, offer another perspective, and strengthen you in your commitment to God. And your presence confirms that the family of God continues, down to the present generation.

# NEW DAYS, NEW WAYS

*" 'These people honor me with their lips,
but their hearts are far from me.' "*

MARK 7:6 NLT

Sometimes a tradition—whether family or personal—stops working for you. You enjoyed it in the past, but you are no longer the same person you were years ago (and neither are others who are carrying on the tradition). It was meaningful once but seems purposeless now. If you feel this way, you are ready to change the tradition, or replace what you're doing with something that better suits your current preferences. God provides traditions to bless your life; and if your tradition no longer blesses, see if it is because He has something new in mind for you to begin.

# Transformation

## NEW YOU

*If anyone is in Christ, he is a new
creation. The old has passed away;
behold, the new has come.*

2 CORINTHIANS 5:17 ESV

Some people reinvent themselves. They take on
a new role, new attitude, and new look, forsaking the person they used to be. With God's Spirit at
work in you, however, you don't need to reinvent
yourself—He is doing it for you. The Holy Spirit is
turning your heart away from self-centeredness and
to God-centeredness. You think more spiritually, act
more kindly, and speak more thoughtfully than in
your earlier life. You are less anxious and more trusting; not nervous, but increasingly confident as you
learn to lean on God. Look in your heart and meet
the gift of your reinvented self!

# TRANSFORMED LIFE

*Faith and works, works and faith,*
*fit together hand in glove.*

JAMES 2:18 MSG

At first, you won't see God's gift of transformation, because it is all on the inside. Soon, spiritual change starts showing on the outside, and it is obvious to everyone. Your language loses words and expressions that are disrespectful to others; you stop going around with people whose values and sense of purpose fall far short of yours; you make more room for God in your life by attending to prayer, study, worship, and fellowship. In short, you are living a transformed life! It is not a onetime thing. What are more observable ways you can keep growing in godly transformation?

# *Truth*

## COMFORTABLE TRUTH

*Buy the truth, and do not sell it, also wisdom
and instruction and understanding.*

PROVERBS 23:23 NKJV

The easiest way to face an uncomfortable truth is to claim that it is only partially true, or true only in certain circumstances. More difficult, but more spiritually profitable, is to wrestle with it until you determine your core beliefs. Concerning the things of God, the issue is this: Does your own reasoning or His Word establish what you accept as true? If your answer is "His Word," then you are willing to admit that there is, indeed, a higher intelligence. You accept the existence of wisdom, beyond any human perception and power. You get comfortable with God—and the truth.

# TRUE FRIENDSHIP

*"You will know the truth,
and the truth will make you free."*

JOHN 8:32 NCV

Your real friends are those who will tell you the truth, even when it is difficult. If they notice something wrong in your life, they broach the subject. If they think you are in danger, they intervene. If they believe you are reluctant to ask for help, they assure you that they are there for you whenever you are ready. Friends take the risk of saying what needs to be said. The truth they tell is a gift far more valuable than anything they may ever give you. God comes with that gift, because He is that kind of friend.

# Values

## HANDLE WITH CARE

*Never let loyalty and kindness leave you!*
*Tie them around your neck as a reminder.*
*Write them deep within your heart.*

PROVERBS 3:3 NLT

Think of things you treasure. You might possess an heirloom you cherish for its meaning; an automobile you appreciate for its practicality; a gem you prize for its significance as well as its price tag. Not one of these things would you handle carelessly, much less forget about! Your Spirit-inspired personal values are things to treasure even more, because they come from the hand of God. Kindness, integrity, truthfulness, and dependability are meaningful, practical, and priceless in your daily walk with God and interactions with others. Handle them with care; never forget you have them—nor who gave them to you.

# LIFE IS BETTER

*"Listen closely to me, and you will
eat what is good; your soul will enjoy
the rich food that satisfies."*

ISAIAH 55:2 NCV

People who live up to their God-given values have it better. Three reasons: One, their decisions are based on lasting values, not on current convenience, emotions, or the influence of popular culture. Two, they gain the trust of others because they are known as honest, truthful, hardworking, and faithful. They hold themselves accountable for their actions and they keep their word. Three, they enjoy the respect of those around them. They are genuine, generous, and joyful. Is your life better because the Holy Spirit has planted in you the gift of godly values? You decide!

# Wisdom

## WISE GUYS (AND GALS)

*If any of you lacks wisdom, you should ask God, who gives generously to all without finding fault, and it will be given to you.*

**JAMES 1:5 NIV**

Many of us hesitate to claim that we are "wise." With a modest blush, we might confess to "smart enough," but that is about it. We will leave the appellation of wisdom to those who answer weighty questions and utter profound thoughts. Yet God pronounces you wise because of the faith you have in Him and the love you hold for Him in your heart. You listen to His counsel, follow where He leads, and rely on Him for your strength and security. Yes, the gift of true wisdom is His to give, and He delights in giving it generously to you.

# HERE'S LOOKING AT YOU

*Don't think that you can be wise merely by being up-to-date with the times. Be God's fool—that's the path to true wisdom.*

1 CORINTHIANS 3:18 MSG

If you are wise in the eyes of your God, you appear just the opposite in the eyes of some people. Put yourself behind their glasses, and imagine how odd your life must look to them! You are not centered on yourself, but on God. You are not possessed by your possessions but use your time, talents, and resources to provide for the needs of others. You don't give in to selfish desires but live satisfied and content. To some people, you seem downright odd, but you only smile and pray that someday, they too will receive the gift of wisdom.

# Words

## SAY AND DO

*You must not say evil things,*
*and you must not tell lies.*

PSALM 34:13 NCV

In the ministry of Jesus Christ, God made His message clear and visible. Jesus spoke words of invitation, forgiveness, healing, and compassion. He also used words to warn and teach, inform and enlighten. Most importantly, He backed up His words with action, showing what kindness, gentleness, correction, and love look like. Then, as now, words are simply words until they are practiced. If there is a gap between the things you say and do, look to Jesus as your example. Receive His fulfilled words as His gifts to you, and watch your practiced words become your gifts to others.

# GOOD WORDS

*Let your conversation be gracious and attractive so that you will have the right response for everyone.*

COLOSSIANS 4:6 NLT

When speaking to friends about spiritual matters, we look for words that can help them understand, offer them insight, and direct them toward a connection to God. For other topics, our words often slip from that lofty standard. We are more focused on lobbing clever comments than in responding from a heart immersed in God's love. It doesn't need to be that way with you. The words of God's forgiveness, compassion, and kindness are not only for spiritual topics, but for all topics. Many of your listeners will never hear God's words, but they will be listening to you.

# *Work*

## GO EASY ON HIM

*The word of God is alive and active.*

HEBREWS 4:12 NIV

If you think you work hard, look at the load God is carrying! Right now, the Holy Spirit is at work in your soul, nurturing the seed of faith He has planted in you. With every God-sent thought you ponder, question you consider, and idea you allow to emerge, He is actively shaping and pruning, cultivating and encouraging spiritual maturity. Through your Spirit-inspired decisions and actions, God is busy revealing to you His plan and purpose for your life. He labors 24/7 to encourage you and keep you close to Him. Help Him out by making His job easy!

# GOOD WORK

*Commit your actions to the LORD,*
*and your plans will succeed.*

PROVERBS 16:3 NLT

Work can overwhelm. When we take our responsibilities seriously, we spend every ounce of energy we possess on getting things right. At the same time, work is a God-given gift. Work provides a sense of purpose and satisfaction, along with tangible and intangible rewards. When you balance the amount of time you spend on work, with loved ones, and alone with God, you can fully appreciate the blessings your work provides. Work is a gift, but not your only gift. There are many besides. It helps to remember that after God created the world, on the seventh day He rested.

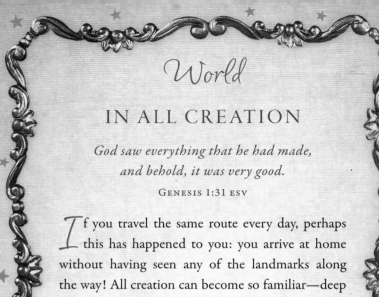

# World

## IN ALL CREATION

*God saw everything that he had made,*
*and behold, it was very good.*

**GENESIS 1:31 ESV**

If you travel the same route every day, perhaps this has happened to you: you arrive at home without having seen any of the landmarks along the way! All creation can become so familiar—deep blue sky, rippling leaves, fragrant flowers—that you fail to notice it anymore. No matter where you are, the sun, moon, and stars are above you. There are rivers and forests, prairies and deserts, meadows and gardens surrounding you; yes, even the bouquet you brought home from the grocery store counts. All creation is God's gift to you. Have you seen any of it today?

# BEST OF THE BEST

*"He will rejoice over you with gladness,*
*He will quiet you with His love,*
*He will rejoice over you with singing."*

ZEPHANIAH 3:17 NKJV

If you love cuddling a beloved pet, cultivating delicate flowers, watching a foamy surf surge against the shore, you are enjoying God's enchanting creation. If you have ever stood in awe at the sight of a brilliant sunset or gazed in wonderment at a star-studded sky, you are admiring the splendors of His earth. If you have ever felt blessed to be right where you are, you know what it is like to give thanks for the gift of His wonderful world. Take note—the same God who created the world has created you, the best of the best of all His work.

# Scripture Index

# NOTES

# NOTES

_____

_____

_____

_____

_____

_____

_____

_____

_____

_____

_____

_____

_____

_____

_____

# NOTES

_____

_____

_____

_____

_____

_____

_____

_____

_____

_____

_____

_____

_____

_____

# NOTES

# NOTES